REVIVAL
our eternal hope

by Glenn Foster

KENDALL/HUNT PUBLISHING COMPANY
4050 Westmark Drive   Dubuque, Iowa   52002

Acknowledgments

A special thanks to the original team in Sweetwater's Publication Department who made the first edition of this book possible: Carla Bruce, Aleta Harrell, Irene Klindworth, and Doris Pakos.

Thanks to Debbie Becker and Carla Bruce for the new layout and the workbook section in this edition.

And thanks to Steven Rutt for providing the quotations at the open of each chapter.

Glenn Foster

The first edition of this book was published in 1986 by Huntington House, Inc. under the title, *Revival or Ruin*.

All Scripture quotations in this book are from the King James Version of the Bible unless otherwise indicated.

Contents

Foreword

All of us know that things are bad and are getting worse in the world, but far too few of us realize that grace abounds where sin abounds. This book looks to God's promise rather than to America's problems. It is positive, scriptural, balanced and desperately needed.

This is a book of hope: hope for the believer, hope for the Church, and hope for the nation. While some Christians are looking for the ultimate hope of Christ's return, this book speaks of the immediate hope of revival in our generation. It offers a needed balance to some of the "doomsday" utterances that are becoming more and more frequent today.

I was stirred, excited and strengthened in reading the manuscript of this book. I had purposed to merely scan it but ended up reading every page, often with tears of thanksgiving in my eyes. I wholeheartedly agree with Glenn Foster that "the best is yet to come."

In my opinion, this book is a "must read" for every believer.

Judson Cornwall, Th.D.

*This timely book will bless and encourage you to believe
God for greater things than you have dared hope for in the past.*

Paul F. Crouch President, Trinity Broadcasting Network

*The reader's heart will be set ablaze not only with personal revival but
also with well-founded hope for the greatest world revival of all time.*

Stephen Strang Editor and Publisher, Charisma Magazine

*In this anointed book, the author has documented
God's plan for revival in this century.*

Freda Lindsay, Christ For The Nations

*This is a book of hope: hope for the believer, hope for the Church,
and hope for the nation. In my opinion, it is a "must read."*

Judson Cornwall, Th.D.

THE HOPE OF REVIVAL

Revival is the ultimate miracle.

Those who walk in the hope of revival enjoy a lifestyle of continuous fulfillment and expectation.

Revival encompasses all of God's works in a single sweep of His hand, leaving in its wake blessings only possible through God's mighty power. Revival is evangelism — stirring the unbeliever to repentance and bringing him to salvation. Revival is renewal — shaking the complacent, lukewarm Christian to get back to the job of building the Kingdom. Revival is recommitment — inspiring God's people to creative new outreach and ministry.

Revival.

Men of faith of all generations who have heard the voice from the Most Excellent Glory, the voice that shakes heaven and earth, have all received the same good report: Be of good cheer. I have overcome the world. I am with you always. I will do a work in your time which, if it were told you, you would not believe. And though the vision tarry, wait for it, for it will be fulfilled in its time. Yes, from the foundations of the world, eyes have not seen and ears have not heard all the things that God has prepared for them that wait upon Him. (John 16:33; Matt. 28:20; Hab. 1:5; 2:3; Isa. 64:4 paraphrased.)

Revival.

Men of faith who have held to the good report and the faith of God have subdued kingdoms, wrought righteousness, and beheld the glory of God sweeping the land in great power and mercy.

Revival.

To speak of revival is to address the greatest contradiction in life. Man's normal order of life is a process of gradual decay which so often buries us in a sense of futility—as the writer of Ecclesiastes says, "Vanity of vanities, all is vanity." The revival lifestyle, which we present in this book, challenges, overcomes and takes away the dark covering of vanity and hopelessness from the mind of man. Therefore, the subject of revival and new life in Christ evokes a contest for the control of man's mind.

The human viewpoint, even of the born again man, is often the downward look that says, "Things start out great but lose their shine all too soon!" The divine viewpoint is the upward look that says, "Because the word of faith is near, there will always be a new supply of life and power in Christ." The divine viewpoint will always cause us to see that revival is possible.

If we, as believers, do not grasp the divine viewpoint, God will step forth in a sovereign move of the Spirit, stand in the gap, and revive His work somewhere in each generation showing with infallible proofs that He is the God of revival — the God of all flesh. No one who yearns for revival will be disappointed. God will not and can not fail to fulfill His plan. His truth marches on in all generations.

Revival is birthed in the chambers of prayer, released on the wings of praise, and raised up where God's people are gathered in unity. Revival comes when men walk in God's ways and follow biblical order; when men receive the good report. And most importantly, revival comes when God's people walk in the glory of His presence.

True revival is the result of man's exposure to God's unveiled presence. Each chapter in this book will bring you into a new understanding of God's ways and glory. The Bible principles found herein will prepare you to walk in the glory of the Lord each day of your life and to be an effective tool in the hand of God to cause revival to continue throughout your lifetime and beyond.

This book has come out of many years of prayer and earnest labor in the gospel. It was written out of a deep conviction that the gospel must yet be preached in its full power and glory throughout the earth before the coming of the Lord. It has become clear to me that total world evangelism is only possible by a totally restored Church, moving in the power of the gospel, fanning revival fires among all nations, kindreds, tribes and languages.

Glenn Foster

The visible kingdom of Satan shall be overthrown, and the kingdom of Christ set up on the ruins of it, everywhere throughout the whole habitable globe....Now the kingdom of Christ shall in the most strict and literal sense be extended to all nations, and the whole earth....there shall be no part of the world of mankind but what shall be covered with the knowledge of God.

Jonathan Edwards, revivalist during the 18th Century Great Awakening; later President of the College of New Jersey, presently called Princeton University

David was not a believer in the theory that the world will grow worse and worse, and that the dispensation will wind up with general darkness and idolatry....The modern notion has greatly damped the zeal of the church for missions, and the sooner it is shown to be unscriptural the better for the cause of God.

Charles H. Spurgeon, *The Treasury of David*, 1874, from an exposition of Psalm 86:9

Expect great things from God.   Attempt great things for God.

William Carey, 1792; English missionary to India; acclaimed as the father of modern missions.

Chapter 1

REVIVAL, GOD'S PLAN FOR WORLD EVANGELISM

God's plan has always been to bring all the nations of every generation to Himself. The frequent recurrence of revival guarantees the fulfillment of that plan. Since the day God fashioned man from the dust of the earth and breathed into him the breath of life, He foresaw in Adam all nations of the earth, and ordained through the death and resurrection of His Son to bring salvation to the ends of the earth.

Never has it been God's will to reap the nations as a grim reaper in judgment. God's plan has always been to win the people of all nations to Himself by His love. This plan can be seen at work throughout the Bible and throughout Church history. His plan remains unchanged. Today, the Holy Spirit is stirring our hearts with a renewed emphasis on Christ's words:

"Go ye into all the world, and preach the gospel to every creature," Mark 16:15; Matthew 28:18-20.

Jesus did not die on the cross by chance; He died according to God's plan, even as it was foretold throughout the Old Testament. The resurrection of Christ on the third day was God's plan from the beginning. Christ arose, not to fulfill the desire of the disciples He had left behind, but to fulfill the command of the eternal word.

God's Plan Began

God's plan began as He prepared the Hebrew people to be the first nation who would be witnesses of God's saving grace. Deuteronomy 32:3, 7-14 shows us how He brought Israel from a desert land, instructed them, nourished them, and caused them to ride on the high places of the earth so that they might publish His name and proclaim His greatness among the nations. The Lord declared in Deuteronomy 32:8 that when He separated the sons of Adam He divided them into nations and set their boundaries according to the number of the children of Israel. And Acts 17:26, referring to this scripture in Deuteronomy, interpreted the intent of this divine arrangement and said that the purpose for dividing the sons of Adam into nations was to make it possible for all nations to be touched with the gospel. This shows me that there was an adequate number of believers in Israel who would be able, if they obeyed God's voice, to bring meaningful witness to every individual among the nations of that time.

The only change in the New Testament era is that through the atonement of Christ God has enlarged His nation of witnesses to include all who believe the gospel. For the gospel-witness was first to and through the Jew. After that, believers from all nations were included in the witnessing team. To this intent Jesus told the Jewish apostles to go into all the world and not only to preach the gospel to every creature, but also to make disciples of all nations, teaching them to observe all that He had commanded. Thereby, these new disciples became a part of the army of the Lord — that great company of overcomers who give witness night and day to God's plan of salvation.

Today, we are part of that great nation of witnesses. We are part of God's plan for our time. And just as His plan has never failed in the past, so it will not fail in our day. Even in times when the Church has lost its spiritual power and seems unable to fulfill the command to go into all the world, God's plan is still in motion. For at the heart of God's plan to bring all the nations of every generation to Himself is the promise of revival. The restoration of the Church is as much a part of God's plan as was the resurrection of Christ. The promise of revival forever remains a part of our inheritance. Revival must come. The harvest fields of the earth must be reaped. As the Church is revived again, the "Go ye" of Jesus will once again become the marching orders of the Church.

Last days (Church age)

Many have completely forgotten the great commission, and have drifted so far from God's plan as to think that only a few will be saved in these last days and the remaining multitudes are ordained to be lost. Misunderstanding the Bible term *last days* has led to the false idea that only a few would be saved at the end of the Church age.

Last days does not mean the same as *last things*. The Bible term *last days* refers to the Church age. *Last things* are those things that take place after the Church age.

My understanding of the last days (the Church age) has increased greatly in recent years. Early in my ministry, I thought that last things were the same as last days. I was so taken up with world conditions that I lost sight of God's plan for world evangelism. When the communists took over China and the missionaries were driven out, it seemed evident that the end of the world was imminent. I mourned because so many doors were closing to the gospel and it seemed that the final night had come upon the Church. Failing to remember that Jesus holds the keys to all doors and opens closed doors at His will, I blindly believed that China's doors were closed to the gospel forever and that the night of final doom had fallen upon China's millions. While I stumbled around in my ignorance, God's plan remained unchanged. God's plan for a new day was still intact, just as it is written in Isaiah 21:11,12: The night comes and also the day. A new day of revival always follows the dark night of sin and bondage.

A new day has indeed come to China! China's doors are once more open to the gospel. The revivals now taking place in China are greater than those that took place before the missionaries were forced to leave thirty years ago. How is that possible?

It is possible because world evangelism depends solely on the eternal Word of God, which is ready to be fulfilled at God's command. World evangelism does not depend on open doors to the Church in America. World evangelism does not depend on governments' being friendly to the gospel. Neither does world evangelism depend on the offerings given at missionary conferences in the United States. When our offerings and missionaries cannot reach people in certain countries, the Word of God is not bound and God will yet find a way for His Word to work mightily in those lands.

All of God's plan will be fulfilled

God revealed to Abraham His plan to win all nations to Himself. First, God told Abraham that His children would live in Egypt four hundred years, which they did. Second, He said that He would give them the land of Canaan for an inheritance, which He did. Third, He said that all nations of the earth would be blessed in Abraham's seed. This last part will be fulfilled as the Church completes the great commission. If the first two parts of this plan were fulfilled the last part will be also.

To fulfill this last part of the word given to Abraham, God established the New Testament Church as His tool. The New Testament Church was established right on schedule and exactly to the word given throughout the Old Testament Scriptures. God revealed more of His plan to Peter, who prophesied that times of refreshing would come upon the Church again and again. This promise guarantees that the Church will be able to complete God's purposes in the earth.

God's plan is secure

God's plan for world evangelism is as secure as was God's plan to give birth to the New Testament Church. No word of God is without the power to fulfill itself. Seeing that God has been able to fulfill His plan in all ages past, we can expect times of refreshing and revival to continue to come upon the Church in our time. The commission to go into all the world and preach the good news to every creature is not an optional plan; it is God's only plan. World evangelism will no doubt reach new heights of fulfillment in our lifetime.

God is ready to pour out His Holy Spirit upon all flesh. It is our place to prepare our hearts; it is God's place to pour out the Spirit. We must prepare our hearts and stand in full assurance of faith, expecting God to do His part. We must not allow any idle thoughts of unbelief to rule our outlook and dim our expectation that the whole world will be evangelized.

God's plan is for all nations

Years ago, I heard it said that most of the people of Africa had rejected the gospel in past generations and therefore were given over to a reprobate mind. Only a few, it was said, would ever be saved. What kind of results would you expect from a missionary sent to Africa who did not believe that many Africans could be saved? Thank God, His Word has not been and cannot be bound by faithless men. God's Word is even now working mightily in Africa as the greatest revival in Africa's history is sweeping the land.

Others said that we cannot expect the Arab and Moslem nations to come to Christ. But God's promise *"I will pour out my Spirit upon all flesh"* includes Arabs and Moslems.

The day is coming when the revelation of the knowledge of the glory of the Lord will cover the earth as the waters cover the sea. Isaiah 11:9; Habakkuk 2:14. This promise includes the Moslem nations. Even now, many Moslem nations are experiencing a great outpouring of the Spirit. Indonesia is a marvelous example of the work of the Holy Spirit upon a Moslem nation. Multitudes have come to Christ as the gospel has been preached there.

Nigeria, Africa, the largest black Moslem nation in the world, has also experienced a great outpouring of the Spirit in recent years as multitudes have come to Christ. But this is just the beginning. More are yet to experience the outpouring of the Holy Spirit just as God has promised. God's plan to cause His presence to come upon those who have never known Him will not fail. Matthew 4:16 will become a reality:

> "*The people which sat in darkness saw great light; and to them which sat in the region and shadow of death, light is sprung up.*"

The present restlessness and upheavals in the Arab nations are signs that God is shaking their kingdoms. As the Spirit of God brings conviction upon Moslem nations, the upheavals will continue until, as in Indonesia and Nigeria, millions turn to Christ.

Our vision for world evangelism must not be limited by human reasoning based on negative world conditions. For, as it is written in Proverbs 29:18, where there is no vision, the people perish. We will go no further than our vision. We must let our vision go as far as Christ's word goes and go into all the world, and preach the gospel to every creature.

Joel's Prophecy

Our hope of worldwide revival in our time will be strengthened as we properly understand Joel, Chapters 2 and 3. These chapters contain many keywords, which, when interpreted as the Bible uses them, enable us to understand God's plan more perfectly. We know that Joel's prophecy is relevant to the Church age, for Peter quoting from it on the day of Pentecost said:

> "*This is that which was spoken by the prophet Joel; And it shall come to pass in the last days, saith God, I will pour out of my Spirit upon all flesh...,*"   Acts 2:16, 17.

After speaking of the outpouring of the Spirit upon all flesh, and of great signs and wonders in the heavens and in the earth, Joel then speaks of "*the great and terrible day of the Lord.*" Joel 2:31. The word *terrible* in this scripture does not mean a dark, gloomy day of judgment, but an awesome day when God does wonderful things for His people. When Peter quoted this prophecy of Joel, he used the word *notable*. Notable carries the idea of a brilliant day of illumination. Surely the great and terrible day of the Lord speaks of times of great revival.

The picture in the opening verses of Joel is that of a nation which had experienced near total destruction. The joy of the Lord was gone. The vine and the trees of the field had ceased bearing fruit. In general, the land mourned because of violence and wickedness that was on every hand, Joel 1:1-12. Because evil was so great in Joel's day he gave a strong word against sin. However, the warning of destruction is only one side of the picture; the other side is the promise of complete restoration. For Joel also said that although the enemy had brought great destruction, yet the Lord would do greater things in restoring all that had been destroyed, Joel 2:20-25.

Today, many are asking how God will restore to us all the years that the enemy has ruled in our land. God's answer is that He will call for a remnant who are empowered with a special anointing to bring deliverance from the oppressing hand of the enemy. We read of this promise in Joel 2:32:

> *"And it shall come to pass, that whosoever shall call on the name of the Lord shall be delivered: for in mount Zion and in Jerusalem shall be deliverance, as the Lord hath said, and in the remnant whom the Lord shall call."*

The remnant

The *remnant* in the Bible are those who have retained the faith during a time of spiritual backsliding and confusion among God's people. God always has those like Samuel who still can hear His voice, and whose hearts will respond in faith and obedience. They spark revival and bring fresh light to God's people.

Moses and Joshua were among the remnant whom the Lord called in their day. Gideon, Samson, and all the judges were among the remnant in their day. David, Solomon, and other kings and priests were among the remnant (or the restorers) from the time of the judges until the time of John the Baptist. Then Jesus, Himself, appeared as the restorer of restorers, the king of the saints, and appointed the apostles and the believers throughout the Church age to continue the work of restoration in every generation.

From the day of Pentecost on, all believers are called to be part of the remnant. Some stand out more than others throughout history. After the death of the apostles, the Church fathers, also known as the reformers, brought great deliverance to multitudes. Today, God is still calling the remnant and anointing them to bring deliverance to the captives and to restore the order of His kingdom among the nations. As the remnant of our day move on with God's plan, so the glory of God will be manifested among the nations in revival power.

The hope of glory

In Colossians 1:27 we read that the delivering power that resides in the remnant is Christ Himself — *Christ in you, the hope of glory.* As Christ walks and talks in us, the same power that brought deliverance in the day of the apostles will be known in our day. All will know that He who is in us is greater than he who is in the world. No wonder Joel calls the day of revival the great and notable day of the Lord — a day when God does wonderful things for His people.

Each wave of revival comes as God calls forth the remnant, and each wave of revival brings increasing fulfillment of the great commission. The remnant are those chosen by the Lord to be the coals of fire that start new revivals.

Valley of Jehoshaphat

As we continue to read Joel's prophecy, in Chapter 3 we see that in those days both the remnant, in whom is deliverance, and people from all nations will be drawn into the valley of Jehoshaphat where God will plead with them. The hope of worldwide revival is unmistakably stated in Joel 3. When we treat this passage in Joel as an allegory, we can easily see that the valley of Jehoshaphat is speaking of those times when the power of God draws multitudes of the unsaved into the kingdom of God. Just as we need not go in person to Mount Calvary to receive Christ as Savior, so the remnant and the multitudes spoken of by Joel do not need to go to a valley in the land of Israel in order to experience the work of Jehovah promised in Joel 3.

The word *Jehoshaphat* means the place where Jehovah sits to judge. The writer of the book of Hebrews shows us that all who come to Christ have not only come to the church of the first-born but also to God, the Just Judge. God, the Just Judge, revealed Himself in the Old Testament in seven Jehovah covenants. Each covenant reveals a distinct aspect of God's provision for His people. Jehovah is God's redemptive covenant name. His redeeming grace is revealed in a special way in each of the seven Jehovah covenants.

- ➤ our provider (Genesis 22:13,14)
- ➤ our healer (Exodus 15:26)
- ➤ our banner (Exodus 17:15)
- ➤ our shepherd (Psalm 23)
- ➤ our righteousness (Jeremiah 23:6)
- ➤ our peace (Judges 6:24)
- ➤ the one who is always with us (Ezekiel 48:35)

In the seven Jehovah covenants, God reveals that He is the answer to every need of every person.

Thus, as we consider this text in the third chapter of Joel, our focus should be upon the nature of Jehovah, the Judge, rather than on the wickedness of the multitudes. God's ever-abiding grace outweighs the sin of man.

Charles Finney, a 19th-Century revivalist said, "Do not tell me of the rising floods of evil, but let me tell you of the rising floods of grace." The darker the night of sin, the brighter the light of God's grace. The greater the number of wicked, the larger the harvest. The historical record of revival in Charles Finney's day shows, beyond doubt, that he spoke the truth of God and properly applied the words of Romans 5:20: *"Where sin abounded, grace did much more abound."* As the grace of God abounded in Finney's day, cities of thousands turned to God overnight. Such a revival is a perfect fulfillment of the promise of Joel 3.

The first fulfillment of Joel's prophecy is recorded in the book of Acts, as the Holy Spirit was poured out on the day of Pentecost. Acts 2. Not only were men gathered in Jerusalem from all nations as Joel had said, but also God had prepared His remnant. There God sat in their midst to plead with men from all nations.

That day, the harvest sickle of the gospel brought in three thousand souls. Later, the multitude was again gathered; on that day, five thousand were brought into the kingdom of God. Again and again, thousands have been brought into the kingdom.

Multitudes hear the gospel

Just what takes place in the valley of Jehoshaphat can be seen in the revival ministry of George Whitefield in the 18th Century. In his day, multitudes, up to fifty thousand at a time, were drawn together in one place to hear the gospel. There, it is said, with thunderous tones that shook the very soul of every man within the sound of Whitefield's voice, God pled with the people and the harvest of souls was reaped.

Every time the multitudes are drawn by the Spirit of God, the Lord sits as judge in their midst and pleads with them to accept Jesus Christ and His atonement for their sins. Even in our time, reports are coming from the Orient, Indonesia, Africa, India and South America, telling of multitudes being drawn together to hear the gospel. On many occasions the crowds are in excess of one or two hundred thousand. Multitudes and multitudes of heathen are gathering and finding deliverance as the remnant declare the good news of the gospel.

There is a marked difference between the day-by-day reaping of a soul here and a soul there, which is personal evangelism, and a valley-of-Jehoshaphat harvest, where multitudes are swept into the kingdom of God in a short period of time, which is mass evangelism. The book of Acts tells of souls being added daily to the Church as well as those special times when multitudes were added in one sweep of the sickle. Both are fulfillments of the great commission.

Today, through radio and television, we do not need to gather multitudes in a stadium, tent, or open field to experience mass evangelism. Today, the remnant can preach deliverance to millions at the same time through the mass media. We have all been thrilled by crusades on television where God's power has been gloriously displayed and where multitudes came to Christ. Surely the day of the Lord — that brilliant glorious day — is bursting upon this generation.

The mighty ones

We read in Joel 3 of God's call to the *mighty ones* to come down to the valley of Jehoshaphat. The mighty ones are the joyful people of faith who have been prepared to reap the harvest.

> *"Assemble yourselves, and come, all ye heathen, and gather yourselves together round about: thither cause thy mighty ones to come down, O Lord."* Joel 3:11.

David was one of those mighty ones who came from the heights of Zion. He was still a young man when the armies of the Philistines were gathered against Israel and the giant, Goliath, flaunted his powers against the army of God, I Samuel 17. But God had been preparing David for this time as he tended his father's flocks and sang songs of praise in the hills of Judea. The hills of Judea speak to us of the high places of praise, where the hearts of men are prepared in faith and hope. It was in such a setting of praise that God prepared David to be a mighty one, able to go against the giants in the land.

As the Lord did in David's day, so today He still calls, "Come down, mighty ones. The harvest is ripe. Come down, Church. Today is your day." When we see *Philistines and giants* in the land, when sin is rampant in the streets, we can know that very soon we will hear the voice of Him that sits upon the throne saying, "Come down, mighty ones. The giants are going to fall in defeat again. And the harvest will be reaped."

For years, there has been a great emphasis on faith and a joyful lifestyle. It is evident on every hand that the Lord is preparing an army of joyful, positive believers who will be ready at His command to come down from the heavenly places of love, joy and peace and into the valley of Jehoshaphat, shining with the posi tive, powerful testimony, "Our God reigns!"

The Great Contradiction

How is it possible for some Christians to view the future as hopeless, placing their emphasis on the increasing immorality and violence in the land, while others speak of hope, restoration, and new waves of glory? How can we have revival now when darkness is apparent on every hand? The answer is found in Isaiah 60:2:

> *"For, behold, the darkness shall cover the earth, and gross darkness the people: but the Lord shall arise upon thee, and his glory shall be seen upon thee."*

On the one hand, we have gross darkness upon some; on the other hand, we have the glory of the Lord upon others. Those who view the future as growing darker and darker see only those who are in darkness. They fail to see the light shining from the kingdom of God — the light that will overcome the darkness. Others, however, understanding God's plan for the salvation of all nations, see the light of the Lord arising upon His people, and know that the darkness can never overcome the light. These are proclaiming a positive message of hope, peace and restoration. These mighty ones expect God to fulfill His word again and again.

> *"The people which sat in darkness saw great light."*
> Matthew 4:16.

Light and darkness coexist

Here we see the principle of coexisting light and darkness. The principle is simple. The darkness grows worse and worse until the light shines from God's people who act as mirrors reflecting the light of God's love into the darkened places of a lost world. Let us consider in a modern-day setting the principle of coexisting light and darkness. Most people would agree that gross darkness is covering the people of the earth today. Newspapers, radio and television constantly tell of the gross, dark deeds that men inflict upon one another. They seem to major in the dark side of the news. Even some Christians seem to see only the dark side of things.

On the other hand the Lord has raised up many great voices of Christian television, radio and the printed page. These report the good news of God's work among the nations. The effect of the good news is already being felt in every quarter of the earth. Millions who were imprisoned in darkness, without hope, have begun to see a greater light. They see on Christian television every day that multitudes are receiving help from the hand of God.

As more and more Christians understand that when gross darkness is upon the nations the glory of the Lord will arise in new power upon His people, hope for earth's multitudes will fill our hearts and we will prepare for the greatest revival in earth's history. Isaiah 60:4 speaks of this:

> *"Lift up thine eyes round about, and see: all they gather themselves together, they come to thee...."*

As we see the multitudes coming we will also see the fulfillment of Isaiah 60:5.

> *"The abundance of the sea shall be converted unto thee, the forces of the Gentiles shall come unto thee."*

Who will come and be converted? Just a few here and there? No. The multitudes of earth — the abundance of the sea — will come. Praise God, it's time for this kind of revival!

Lift up your head, missionary; see them coming! Lift up your head, pastor, evangelist, church worker; see them coming! This word of Isaiah 60:5 must come to pass. Never has there been a more timely day.

What would happen if all Christians stopped viewing the darkness as a sign of the end of the world, but saw it as the sign of the beginning of the greatest revival in history? What an immediate difference it would make if we would believe that now is the time for the mighty ones to come down into the valley of Jehoshaphat and confront the darkness with the light of the Lord. Would not the result be a pushing back of the darkness that covers men? Would not the penetrating light of the gospel of Jesus Christ shine into the hearts of the multitudes? And would not we see worldwide revival now?

Throughout history, God has called many mighty ones to overcome the darkness of this world with the brightness of His glory. If we think back over this century, we can see how often the world has come to the brink of destruction. But God has always intervened and deliverance has come to the multitudes. Again and again, the word of the Lord has gone forth and God has said to the heathen, "Your wickedness is great." Yet the world has *not* come to an end. For when the vats of wickedness overflow then it is time once again for the vats of grace to overflow, lest the world be consumed with a curse. (See Joel 3:13; Romans 5:20,21; Malachi 4:5,6.)

Perilous times

A New Testament text that shows us the principle of light overcoming darkness is found in II Timothy 3. A study of this chapter will strengthen our hope for revival in our time. The text begins, *"In the last days, perilous times will come."* It then gives a descriptive list of the evils in men's hearts that make these times so perilous:

> *"... lovers of their own selves, covetous, boasters, proud, blasphemers, disobedient to parents, unthankful, unholy, without natural affection, trucebreakers, false accusers, incontinent, fierce, despisers of those that are good, traitors, heady, highminded, lovers of pleasure more than lovers of God; having a form of godliness, but denying the power thereof."*

When will these perilous times come? In the last days (which is the Church age). Some seem to think that all the evils mentioned in II Timothy 3 just began to appear in our generation, and that, as a result, we have no hope of a new revival in our time. Thus, it is thought by some that the world will get worse and worse until Jesus comes and takes out His few remaining saints.

But this text does not teach us that the *world* will get worse and worse, thereby making revival impossible. According to verse 13, it is the *seducers* and *evil men* who will not repent that will grow worse and worse. We read in verse 8 that men and seducers who resist the truth are reprobate concerning the faith and they are compared by Paul to Jannes and Jambres, the false prophets who withstood Moses in Old Testament times. And we see in verse 9 that these seducers and evil men will proceed no further, for their folly will be manifest unto all men. They ultimately come up against the light of God and are stopped in their tracks.

When the mighty ones arise and shine in the valley of the Lord, the light of God shining from their lives is as a great wall standing in the way of evildoers, so that they cannot continue to deceive others with their evil practices. The wicked and ungodly may be marching in the streets today boasting of their evil ways, but a day will soon come when they will be stopped by God's wall of light and glory.

Thus we see how the light of God sets free those who believe, while, at the same time, it stops those who do not believe. Jannes' and Jambres' power to deceive others was cut off as their lies and deceptions were exposed by the light and truth spoken by Moses as he declared the word of the Lord to Pharaoh and showed the miracles of God to all of Egypt. Exodus 7-14.

Examples from recent history also show this Bible principle at work when evil men come against the light of the gospel. During one of Sister Woodsworth Etter's tent meetings in a Midwestern city in the late 19th Century, a band of hoodlums came with the intention of disrupting the meeting. As they started to make their move, they were slain under the power of God. The wall of light was too great to resist. Later, as they arose, one by one they confessed their sins and called upon the Lord. They confessed that, although they had come to disrupt the meeting, the glory of God had delivered them and changed their lives.

The power and glory of the gospel is not manifested when the gospel is preached under the influence of a negative, humanistic mind. But when the Lord calls His mighty ones to a confrontation with the forces of darkness, Jesus will go before them, confirming the Word with signs and wonders, and giving birth to mighty revivals in the earth. These mighty ones are also called the army of the Lord in the book of Joel: God will utter His voice before His army, Joel 2:11. He will roar out of Zion and utter His voice from Jerusalem, and the earth will shake before His great army, Joel 3:16. Truly, the earth will shake as the nations come down to the valley of Jehoshaphat.

As God continues to bring the multitudes into the valley of Jehoshaphat, we can expect greater waves of revival to be poured out upon the earth. According to Haggai 2:9, the glory of the latter house will be greater than that of the former. Each move of God will be greater than the previous. And for us who are alive today, now is the time to experience the greater glory.

The glory of the latter house

Mary Goforth Moynan, daughter of Jonathan Goforth, a well-known missionary to China in the earlier part of this century, spoke at our church. She told of being invited to China and of returning to the place of her early childhood. How surprised she was to find that the government of China was returning the churches to the people. She was even more surprised to find two old men who had been teachers in her father's Bible school years before. Those men had survived the thirty years of persecution of the church in China and are now living witnesses of a new revival in our day.

When I heard this story, I realized that it was the promise of Haggai 2:3 at work, keeping these old men alive so that they might see the restored house of glory. Truly, the glory of the latter house in China today is much greater than that of the former. Before the government of China shut down open church meetings and forced the missionaries to leave, there were known to be about ten million believers in China. Today, there are at least thirty million. Both the older returning missionaries to China and the elderly believers still there are eyewitnesses of the great Bible principle that the glory of the latter house will be the greatest, and that God will always have those who can testify to that fact.

We need not fear the gross darkness upon the nations, for the light of the Lord will yet shine upon them, just as Isaiah 60:2 promises. We need not fear the power of evil men and seducers, for they will be stopped as God's people arise and shine, just as II Timothy 3:9 promises. Let us lift our vision higher until our vision for world evangelism embraces everything that God included in His plan from the foundation of the world. Let us prepare for the mightiest revival in earth's history.

It is written:

➤ I will pour out my Spirit upon all flesh.

➤ I will restore.

➤ I will fulfill.

➤ I will complete my work upon the earth.

Therefore, let us say, Amen and amen. Let us walk in the lifestyle of the miraculous and be a part of the army of the Lord fulfilling the great commission.

Questions for this chapter are on page 195

What is God's Kingdom? By His Holy Spirit to act and rule over His own people that in all their works the riches of His goodness and His mercy may clearly stand out. . . . This Kingdom flourishes—spiritual, incorruptible, eternal.

John Calvin from *The Piety of John Calvin*

Oh! Spirit of God, bring back thy Church to a belief in the gospel! The gospel must succeed . . . it cannot be prevented from succeeding; a multitude that no man can number must be saved.

Charles H. Spurgeon, 1834–1892, sermon
from Metropolitan Tabernacle Pulpit

The world is (so to speak) renewed by Christ . . . even now we are in the progress and accomplishment of it . . . The prophet has in his eye the whole reign of Christ, down to its final close, which is also called 'the day of renovation and restoration.'

John Calvin, commentary on John 13:31

Though our persons fall, our cause shall be as truly, certainly and infallibly victorious, as that Christ sits at the right hand of God. The gospel shall be victorious. This greatly comforts and refreshes me.

John Owen, a leading theologian in England, addressing the
House of Commons on October 1651.

The year of the revival of primitive Christianity in the power of it, will be the year of the redeemed . . . When the bounds of the church will be enlarged by the conversion of Pagan and Mohometan nations to the faith of Christ, and the spreading of the gospel in foreign parts.

Matthew Henry, New Year's Day 1707

Chapter 2

THE HOLY SPIRIT
AT WORK THROUGHOUT HISTORY

The prophet Malachi wrote: *"I am the Lord, I change not."* The word given to Moses was, *"I am that I am... and this is my memorial to all generations"* Centuries later, the writer of Hebrews grasped the same vision as he wrote, *"Jesus Christ the same yesterday, and today, and forever."*

Revival in our generation is a must, not only because of man's need, but also because Jesus Christ *must* pour out of His Spirit again and again upon every generation as He poured it out on the apostles in the first century. The fact that God is unchangeable requires that a way be made for His glory to be known among men of every generation.

The greatest stories of history are not those that tell of wars, cultural developments, architectural accomplishments, or works of art. The stories in which we find the most beneficial and lasting effects on society are to be found in the accounts of the great revivals of history.

Historical Review

A review of past revivals, going back to the earliest record of Scripture, gives us insight concerning God's dealings with His people to bring the Church to peak performance.

The judges

In the Book of Judges, we find a comparable setting to the moral and spiritual condition of our generation. We also find a clear pattern showing God's plan to continually offer man a hope of renewal and restoration of spiritual life and strength in the scriptural record of the revivals sent by God through the ministry of the judges.

As God raised up leaders who were filled with the power of the Almighty, the results were always the same: False religion, such as Baal worship was destroyed. True worship of God was restored, as the people learned again to walk in God's ways. The armies of God, though often far outnumbered, became mighty in the Spirit, and drove the oppressors out of the land. And, most importantly, once righteousness was restored, the government of God established, and the oppressors driven out, a long period of peace and prosperity followed—in some cases in some cases forty years, Judges 3:11, 5:31, 8:28. In one case eighty years of peace followed the revival, Judges 3:30.

The lesson of the Book of Judges is clear. Believers in every generation can experience revival.

➤ We can see the government of God established in society.

➤ We can see the oppressing armies of the earth pushed back into the narrowest corners of the earth.

➤ We can see long periods of peace and tranquillity among the nations wherein the people of God can build up the kingdom of God and occupy until the Lord comes as He has commanded us to do.

In the Scriptures we find chapter after chapter describing the struggle between good and evil, while a single verse, and sometimes only one line of verse, tells of the victory and the long periods of peace that followed, such as Judges 3:11: *"And the land had rest forty years."* For those who believe, as Abraham believed, a one-line word of faith can open the gates to a lifetime of peace and prosperity in the kingdom of God. On the other hand, for those who struggle, finding it difficult to believe the good report, it takes chapter after chapter, seeing the same story told again and again in different forms, to settle the heart in faith.

Every book of the Bible, from Genesis to Revelation, gives the same story. When man walks in the flesh, the devil lords over him with sin, sickness and a miserable lifestyle. For the man who believes God and walks in His ways, allowing His government to be established in his heart, quite the opposite is true. God has promised to prosper everything that such a man puts his hand to do. Thus the man who walks in faith will walk in the lifestyle of revival.

It seems evident that when God raises up ministries that emphasize the positive promises of Scripture, the people rally and faith rises like a mighty river. Long years of struggling with sin and unbelief are overcome, and revival continues so long as men seek the Lord with all their hearts. The recurrence of revival can be seen from Genesis to this generation.

The First Great Awakening

While many revivals occurred in earlier times, the revival of the 16th century began a work of renewal and restoration that will not cease until the full glory of the apostles' day is restored and the great commission is exhaustively fulfilled. God has promised that the heavens will retain Jesus until the time of the restoration spoken of by the mouth of all the holy prophets, Acts 3:21.

Step by step, and century by century, God has restored increasing degrees of light and glory to the Church. The Church of this hour has much to gain by looking back and considering the work of God in past centuries. The Church of the 20th century does not stand on its own merits. Believers of our time may walk in an on-going revival lifestyle only because of God's mighty works in revivals of past centuries.

The historic record of revival is an ever-shining light for all generations to come. Each revival has brought a new emphasis on the Word of God and the personal relationship between the believer and his Lord. Every revival adds, in one way or another, to the believer's ability to live a victorious life.

A brief look at several major revivals of the past shows that each revival left a new deposit of kingdom authority and the light of divine wisdom, which has led man further and further away from the black night of dead religion that ruled the earth in the Dark Ages.

Today, after generations of ever-increasing light and glory, it is difficult for us to comprehend the utter darkness of the Dark Ages. For centuries the peasants of the European Continent had been subjected to the absolute sovereign rule of the wealthy and powerful in both the church and the state. Sometimes these overlords worked together to further their purposes; other times they worked against one another in their separate attempts to grasp still more power. Either way, the masses suffered. Bound under a tyrannical religious and political system that stifled the life-flow of God's grace to the human race, the masses remained poor, uneducated and spiritually oppressed.

Martin Luther

Martin Luther was a revivalist who lived in Germany in the 16th Century. Truly, darkness was upon the earth and gross darkness upon the people in his day. But once again the eternal God of glory, who commanded the light to shine in the beginning, found a vessel through whom His glory could be revealed.

Luther's ministry in the early part of the 16th Century came as a shining light of spiritual truth. This new revival of truth came two centuries after the beginning of the Renaissance, a time in which there was a reviving of art, literature and learning in Europe. The Renaissance, however, was not a reviving of spiritual truth; it was the reviving of the liturgy of a dead orthodoxy and a rebirthing of ancient philosophy, art and culture based on Greek humanism, much like secular humanism in our day.

Justification by faith

Martin Luther was stirred by the Spirit of God to see the truth as it is in Jesus, and equipped with the mighty example of the apostolic age, he began to preach "justification by faith." Multitudes were swept into an apostolic-like revival in the years that followed. Truly, as it was said of the apostles, "These men have turned the world upside down," so it must be said of Luther's ministry in the 16th Century.

As Luther began his ascent out of the pits of humanism and the futility of dead religious practice, the Church was set on a path that grew steadily brighter with each new wave of revival. From Luther's day until today, the Holy Spirit has been outpoured from time to time, bringing light and faith to the hearts of millions throughout the earth over the centuries. Each new revival has not only brought greater understanding of God's plan for the salvation of the nations, but also new tools to spread the gospel to the uttermost parts of the earth.

Several remarkable works of God were accomplished during the revival in Luther's day, and they have continued until now. One important work was that the humanistic philosophy, which established man's own mind as his ultimate judge, was overthrown and the Word of God was established as the ultimate judge of right and wrong.

The printing press

Another great work accomplished during Luther's revival was the translation of the Word of God into the everyday language spoken by the common man. Luther and his associates made full use of the printing press and spread revival as they printed more Bibles, hymns, tracts, cartoons and pamphlets in a four year period than in any other four years of German history to this day.

The restoration of the Church and the resulting restructuring of society that began in Luther's day spread across Europe during the 16th Century. Since that time millions have been brought to Christ worldwide over the centuries through the testimony of churches birthed from this restoration movement.

John Calvin

John Calvin, who was born in France, also lived in the 16th Century, and was greatly influenced by Martin Luther's teachings. The revival under Calvin's ministry was centered in Geneva, Switzerland and spread during his lifetime to Holland, France, and other European countries. John Calvin was so aflame with the fire of revival that he pictured the symbol of his ministry to be the heart of man held up to God, burning with the fire of holy zeal.

Christian community

Calvin's ministry established further biblical concepts which have continued to bear influence on society. One was the creation of a Christian community in which there was no monarch. There, both Church and civil magistrates were subject to the Word of God. Thus Geneva, Switzerland became a tiny island of freedom surrounded by nations ruled by despots. This city became a refuge for believers from other countries who were being persecuted and killed because of their new-found faith. Some historians have gone so far as to call Geneva the "first Puritan church" and the "nursery for democracy." As time went by, this Christian community concept was used by many Puritans who fled England and other European countries in order to establish Christian communities in the New World.

Systematic doctrines

Another of Calvin's lasting contributions to the Church and to society was the establishment of clear teachings of systematic doctrines. These teachings came about as Calvin answered, from the Bible, allegations against the Reformation. Calvin's systematic teachings gave the common man safe boundaries in which to interpret the Scriptures. These systematic teachings, however, were more than a safeguard to help keep the believer in sound Bible doctrine. Calvin's doctrines became the guidelines that ruled out the humanistic philosophy of past centuries, providing, for the first time in history, a complete systematic study of Scripture. Calvin's works were unique in that they were based *only* on the Scriptures.

Today, we can look back and see that Calvin's doctrines were like the strings on a violin, giving every believer equal opportunity to live a harmonious life of faith. Since that time, Bible-believing people have enjoyed a more or less harmonious sound. Although each revival may have emphasized its own unique aspect of truth, these fundamental doctrines of Scripture have remained the chords that have sounded revival for every generation from Calvin's time until today.

Every new wave of revival built upon the previous one and raised the church to new heights.

John Knox

As John Knox, a young man from Scotland, came under the influence of the reformation work of Luther and Calvin, the revival fires continued to spread in the 16th Century. John Knox saw himself as a prophet blowing the trumpet in Zion. As new translations of the Bible emerged in the languages of the common man, Knox preached forcefully throughout Scotland that the kingdom of God was at hand. Under his ministry, the nation of Scotland was transformed practically overnight. The nation turned from two percent church attendance to ninety-eight percent attendance as thousands were swept into the kingdom of God. This massive revival of the 16th Century established forever the fact that God can pour out His Spirit and send a revival in any generation regardless of how dark things may be.

The ministry of the prophet

Knox's ministry also established as a fundamental rudiment of biblical theology that it is the ministry of the prophet and the Church to speak to governments and kings, making known the word of the Lord concerning the just rule of governments.

The ministry of John Knox also bore heavily on the thinking of many Puritans, who later established the American form of democracy with the bonding theme "One nation under God." Knox's ministry demonstrated the perfect accord between Church and state when the state is merely an instrument to govern justly among men under God.

The revival under John Knox's ministry also bore further fruit in caring for the poor and needy. Thus, the Church became much more than a pulpit for sounding out theological statements. Tens of thousands of believers sprang up from this revival whose influence spread over several generations.

King James Bible

In preparation for the next great wave of revival, God moved on King James of England to have the Bible translated into the English language. This new translation was heavily based on the unfinished work of William Tyndale, who had been martyred in 1535, and who had translated most of the Bible into English. The new translation was completed in 1611 and was known as the King James Version. It has become the most widely printed book in history, carrying with it the force and power of revival to the ends of the earth. Truly, where the Bible goes, revival goes.

John Bunyan

Although England had been greatly affected by the revivals of the previous century, religious intolerance still remained. Near the time of the landing of the Pilgrims at Plymouth Rock, John Bunyan was born in England. While Bunyan's preaching brought great revival in England, his greatest influence on the church in his time and to this day has been through his book, *Pilgrim's Progress,* a classic.

Freedom of religion

Bunyan's ministry added to the efforts to bring total freedom of religion. It became abundantly clear in his generation that the preacher must be free from ecclesiastical and state interference. Bunyan spent many years in jail for preaching the gospel, but eventually the laws that had imprisoned him were overthrown.

As we trace the work of the Holy Spirit in revival from that time, we see the gradual development of more and more liberty to preach the gospel. While it remained true that the people of organized, traditional churches still had a tendency to persecute and even attempted often to silence the voice of those bringing a new revival, from that time on, in England, governmental power to stop the spread of revival was minimized.

The record of John Bunyan's life clearly shows how God often chooses the weak things of this world to confound the wise. Bunyan was not only raised in a godless home, but he was also illiterate. His wife taught him to read and led him to the Lord. It is said that the only book he read was the Bible, yet he became the author of 53 books, which were translated into over 100 languages.

Pilgrim's Progress

Pilgrim's Progress has been called by many literary critics "the miracle of English literature." Though Bunyan was virtually illiterate, his writings have been placed with the great authors of history, and one critic said that although Bunyan's English was the simplest and homeliest form ever used by any great English writer, his writings were among the top writings for their polemical, expository, allegorical, straight narrative, autobiographic and poetic styles.

Some of the greatest documents ever penned by man, other than the Bible, have followed in the wake of John Bunyan's influence. These great documents include many hymns, endless volumes of Christian literature, and The Constitution of the United States of America.

George Whitefield

When George Whitefield came on the scene in the early 18th century, the churches in England had lost most of the fervor common to earlier revivals. Form and ritual replaced spiritual zeal. The new generation, for the most part, was lost in its sins. Through Whitefield's preaching, the renewed emphasis on the grace of God caused revival to sweep across England. Whitefield preached over eighteen thousand sermons during his lifetime. His meetings were attended by tens of thousands with multitudes turning to the Lord. The revival fires under this great orator spread throughout England, Scotland, Wales and America. He also made seven trips across the Atlantic to minister in the colonies.

Large crowds

During his thirty-five years of ministry, Whitefield preached to the largest crowds ever known to gather in open air assemblies. On occasion he served communion to as many as fifty thousand in open air services. Most importantly, his message established forever that the grace of God is the all-important emphasis of the gospel.

The greatest evidence of the grace of God at work in Whitefield's day was the outpouring of God's love upon the tens of thousands of illiterate, oppressed and underprivileged people outside of the state church. These people had not been accepted in the churches, nor had any effort been made to reach them with the message of the gospel or to improve their lot in life.

John Wesley

Three years after Whitefield began preaching, John Wesley joined forces with him. The message of the grace of God continued to spread throughout England as Wesley proclaimed the "acceptable year of the Lord," Luke 4:18,19. During this time of revival, the first Sunday schools were established as an energetic program to educate the illiterate.

John Wesley, as did Whitefield, preached to crowds of thousands. At times as many as ten thousand fell under the convicting power of God. During Wesley's ministry, the grace of God swept across England. Using the systematic teaching developed by Calvin, Wesley preached the Word of God, emphasizing the grace of God as well as sanctification and a holy, godly life.

During Wesley's 53 years of ministry, he traveled 180,000 miles throughout England on horseback. As he traveled Wesley fanned the flames of revival, stirred men with the purifying fire of truth, established Sunday schools, and urged believers to not only hold to sound doctrine, but also to apply systematic theology in a meaningful way in their daily lives.

Sunday schools established

Wesley's era of revival added to the over-all restoration of the church through the establishment of Sunday schools, orphanages, and other means by which the practical needs of the people could be met.

Some say that these people were called "Methodists" because they were continually finding new methods for getting the job done.

While the Wesleyan revival was molding the future of England, the colonies were experiencing what is now known as the First Great Awakening in America. The revival in the colonies came under the ministry of Jonathan Edwards and George Whitefield.

Jonathan Edwards

Jonathan Edwards' preaching exposed sin with a deep cutting edge. His most famous sermon, "Sinners in the Hands of an Angry God," is still considered a classic. This sermon brought such response from the Holy Spirit that men under conviction, seeing the very flames of hell lapping around them actually grabbed hold of the pillars of the church while repenting of their sins. During that time, the revival fires spread throughout New England and, through Whitefield, penetrated into the South.

Constitution of the United States of America

Both Jonathan Edwards and George Whitefield greatly influenced the men who would later meet in Philadelphia to frame The Constitution of the United States of America. Benjamin Franklin and others were known to be admirers of Whitefield. Franklin even printed some of Whitefield's journals.

Colleges established

During the first great awakening, the revival was among the ministers, the churches, the public at large, and included those who became the members of our first constitutional government. Many colleges were established during this era which were centers of biblical study. Harvard was established as early as 1636. Yale was established in 1701, and Princeton in 1746. History records that every aspect of society was touched by this revival.

Many more waves of revival, too numerous to mention by name, swept across the young emerging nation. Again and again, the hand of God guided the development of this nation.

The record of history clearly reveals a pattern which illustrates that God is continually at work in the affairs of men to guarantee that there will never be a day when it can be said that God's kingdom is dead.

In the book of Daniel, a great prophecy was given which included all generations to follow. The prophecy said that Jesus would receive an everlasting kingdom and all kingdoms and dominions would serve Him, Daniel 2:44. Thus, the ultimate purpose for the establishment of any nation or kingdom is that it might be a tool in the hand of God to spread His kingdom at appointed times of the Father.

Timothy Dwight

Many years after Jonathan Edwards graduated from Yale University, the school turned from its godly beginnings and was no longer a center of biblical study. Once again, we can see how God always sticks to His plan to intervene during times of spiritual decline. In 1795 a new revival began to break out under the ministry of Timothy Dwight, the grandson of Jonathan Edwards. Timothy Dwight was president of Yale University at that time, and he was so moved upon by the Spirit of God, seeing the deplorable and humanistic state of affairs, that he brought the whole school together and delivered a series of teachings on the nature and danger of infidel philosophy. The effect was immediate and massive. By 1800, the school had completely returned to biblical Christianity. The revival of that day laid the foundations for four more waves of revival during the opening decades of the 19th Century.

Second Great Awakening

Charles Finney

The Second Great Awakening in America came in the 19th Century. Among those used of God to reawaken the nation to its Christian heritage was Charles Finney. During his ministry, entire cities on the East Coast were swept into the kingdom of God. At one point, it was said that his altar was 500 miles long and his converts were 50,000 a day. It is recorded that in one city in New York state 250,000 came to Christ in a two-year period. It is also said that

Atlantic City and other nearby cities experienced such a revival that everyone came to the Lord except for a handful that left town.

During this awakening, the newspapers in many cities daily published the names of those who were turning to Christ instead of writing the obituary columns.

One of Finney's quotes bears repeating here. On one occasion, when someone asked him how he could expect a revival when there was so much evil abounding in the world, he replied:

> "Do not tell me about the rising floods of evil; rather let me tell you about the rising floods of grace."

Finney's ministry established forever, as a clear and definite part of sound theology, that the increasing evidence of evil in the earth is not a sign to the believer that the end of the world is at hand and the harvest of souls is over. Just the opposite is true. When men's sins and wickedness have become as mountains in the earth, God has promised in these last days of grace to establish the house of the Lord on the top, above the mountains of evil, Isaiah 2:2. God also promised in the words of Nahum 1:5 that every mountain of sin and evil would melt down at His presence.

The Civil War

This Second Great Awakening included the time of the Civil War. Generally, when we hear of the Civil War, we hear only of the dark and ugly part of this nation's history. On the other side, though, is the all-important fact that thousands turned to the Lord in both the North and the South.

Spurgeon and Moody

Revival fires continued to burn in the last half of the 19th century under the powerful ministries of Charles Spurgeon in England and D. L. Moody in America. During this time, the Spirit of God was manifested as in the days of the Wesley brothers, as many fell to their knees under the conviction of God. It is recorded that in D.L. Moody's ministry God's power was seen not only in the churches, but on occasions when he went to speak to people on their jobs in the factories many would fall under the power of conviction and receive Christ.

The 19th Century came to a close with a great flurry of God's power, giving the Church of that generation high hope that the 20th Century would be the greatest century in the history of the Church.

Questions for this chapter on page 197

Revival After Revival
the Scope of God's Influence on Mankind Increases

Bibles printed in the everyday language of the people. Preaching God's Word—not philosophy	Luther 16th Century	Justification by faith
First systematic study based totally on Scripture—became the guidelines that ruled out humanistic philosophies	Calvin 16th Century	Biblical principles become the basis for civic government in Geneva, Switzerland
Free exercise of religion without governmental interference	Knox 16th Century	Role of prophet to speak to government
First Sunday schools and orphanages become common to the church	Wesley, Whitefield, Edwards 18th Century	Christian life based on the grace of God evidenced in a pure lifestyle
Lay prayer groups become source for revival power	Finney, Moody, Spurgeon; Lanphier—lay minister 19th Century	Entire communities brought into the kingdom of God
Soul-winning that crosses all denominational, racial & social lines and barriers	Individual revivalists (e.g. Billy Graham) 20th Century	Largest churches ever assembled in history

Revitalized church firmly established in sound doctrine, completing the harvest of the earth

This chart shows the increasing scope of revival throughout the history of Western Civilization, beginning in Martin Luther's time.

Jesus Christ the same yesterday, and today, and forever.

Hebrews 13:8

And the variation again is to be explained solely in terms of the sovereignty of the Spirit. This is supported and substantiated by the history of revivals . . . generally at the beginning of any new work, something unusual does happen . . . the period of the Reformation . . . missionary work in China . . . .

D.M. Lloyd-Jones, *The Sovereign Spirit*

Looking back across the nearly two thousand years that have passed since the coming of Christ we can see that there has indeed been marvelous progress. This process will ultimately be completed, and before Christ comes again we shall see a Christianized world.

Loraine Boettner, Theologian

The fact is that you will not work for the transformation of society if you don't believe society can be transformed. . . It was the utter confidence in the victory of the Christian faith that gave courage to the early missionaries, who fearlessly strode into the farthest reaches of pagan Europe as if they were at the head of an army . . .

David Chilton, *Paradise Restored*

Chapter 3

NEVER-ENDING REVIVAL

The 20th Century opened with a clear and definite display of God's power as revivals swept across the earth, bringing a new emphasis on the work of the Holy Spirit. Tens of thousands were touched anew with the reality that the risen Christ was still present in power on the earth. This fresh outpouring of the Holy Spirit came, for the most part, outside the walls of organized religion. The mighty God who said, "The earth is the Lord's and the fulness thereof," simply stepped out of the box created by organized religion and moved by His Spirit to touch thousands of hungry souls.

20th Century Awakening

Out of this 20th Century awakening, a mighty army began to appear as many new denominations were formed. Thousands gathered around the banners of these denominations that were declaring new hope for the people of this century. A 30 year period of building churches and strengthening denominational lines followed.

During the first part of the 20th Century, revivalists such as R.A. Torrey, Smith Wigglesworth, Doctor Charles Price, Aimee Semple McPherson, and others too numerous to list here, not only experienced mighty demonstrations of the power of God in their generation, but they foretold an even greater work that God would do in the generations to follow.

Smith Wigglesworth

In 1935 Smith Wigglesworth prophesied over David du Plessis, declaring to him that he would live to see the reviving of the old-line denominations. He said that new waves of revival would sweep through the old-line denominations in such dimension that previous revivals of the 20th Century would seem small in comparison. Throughout the 1960s and 1970s, multitudes in the historic churches experienced a fresh awakening as this prophecy began to be fulfilled.

Charles Price

Doctor Charles Price, whose ministry spanned the 1920s through the 1940s, prophesied of a healing revival that would come after his death. According to the prophecy, this healing revival would prepare the way for another major awakening. In the coming revival, Price said, the power of God would move in all who believed, not just in those who were well-known.

I am an eyewitness to many of the mighty works of God in this century. Having seen many demonstrations of God's power as a child, my spirit was stirred early in life to both know the heavenly vision of revival in our time and to follow its unfailing light. While yet a teenager, I grasped an understanding that the best was yet to come. By the Spirit of God, I believed that new and greater waves of revival would sweep across the Church in my lifetime — and that men of faith, moving with God, would build the largest churches in history.

Billy Graham

In the early 1950s, when many thought the days of revival were past, Billy Graham appeared in Los Angeles ministering in the power of the Spirit. In the years that have followed, millions around the world have felt the impact of the Holy Spirit through Billy Graham's ministry as multitudes have received Christ as Savior. Throughout most of the 1950s and 1960s, God raised up many ministries in which Jesus Christ was revealed to millions in new demonstrations of the power of God.

Jesus People

The latter 1960s throughout the 1970s were times of one wave of revival coming upon another as the Spirit of God continued to lay the foundations for the greatest revival in history. The Jesus People movement had its impact throughout the whole nation in the 1960s.

Charismatic Movement

During the 1970s, the Charismatic Renewal not only touched every major denomination, bringing new life and new interest in the work of the Holy Spirit, but tens of thousands of new churches were raised up seemingly overnight. Some of the largest ministries in the history of the Church have been raised up in the last two decades, with television ministries being at the top of the scale in the new revival of our time. In the last ten years, millions of people have come to Christ through Christian television.

In these closing years of the 20th century, we can expect the revival to continue gaining momentum in every corner of the earth. As God awakens and empowers the Church to grasp the opportunity that lies before us in this generation, more and more will turn in faith to Christ. The revival pattern of the past five centuries is obvious — one wave of glory follows another, and each wave strengthens that which has gone before, giving us increased understanding of God's ways and of His greatness in all the earth.

The strength of our hope for revival to continue in our time is ultimately based on God's ability to do what He said He would do. God has gained the reputation throughout the centuries as being a loving, faithful Creator who is able to make Himself known as the God of salvation, the God who is mighty to deliver the people of earth from sin, darkness and bondage.

God's Glory

The prophet Isaiah said that the glory of the Lord would be revealed and that all flesh would see it together. Habakkuk said that the knowledge of the glory of the Lord would cover the earth as the water covers the sea, Habakkuk 2:14. Also see Isaiah 11:9. To speak of the glory of the Lord covering the earth is to say that His great and mighty reputation will be made known among all the people of the earth. People in all nations will know who God is and what He is able to do. These promises hold great meaning for our generation.

No generation before ours has had the tools which would make it possible for all nations to see God's mighty works of love and power openly displayed. But today we have Christian publications, radio and television. It is not uncommon to turn on a television set and see crowds of people praising and worshiping God. The Church of this hour is now grasping the greatness of our Lord and making His glory known throughout the earth.

The question must be asked by all concerned believers: If we have the tools to reach the world in our generation, can we do it by our most sincere efforts alone? Or will we need more than natural tools to get the job done? If we in our generation are to experience revival in the same magnitude as the apostles did in their day, people must again be confronted with the same manifestations of God's glory, power and love.

The Bible frequently speaks of God's shining glory. This refers to the presence of God that shines forth, touching men and changing the course of their lives. David's prayer in Psalm 80 was for God to shine forth and restore His people and to cause His face to shine so that they would be saved.

Many examples are found in the Scriptures of times when God came to the aid of a needy man and touched him with His divine presence. The divine touch, such as Jacob received the night he wrestled with the angel, always changes the course of a man's life and brings spiritual renewal. God became known through Jacob's life as a God who both makes and keeps His covenants and who shows mercy upon thousands.

Moses' time

In the time of Moses, mighty demonstrations of God's presence and power brought millions out of bondage and changed the course of history forever. God's reputation as a God who always intervenes to help man was established even more as He daily fed Israel with manna, gave them water out of the rock, preserved their clothes and shoes, and covered them with a cloud by day and a pillar of fire by night, guaranteeing the continuing work of revival.

Joshua's time

In Joshua's time God's ability to continue His work in an even greater way in a new generation was clearly demonstrated. In an open display of God's power, the river Jordan rolled back at floodstage and Israel crossed over on dry ground. All the inhabitants of the promised land "saw" the glory of the Lord. They did not see the light of His presence with their natural eyes, but they all heard what the God of Israel was able to do. As Joshua and the people advanced toward Jericho, the inhabitants immediately shut their gates and hid within their walls because the reputation of the God of Israel had gone before His people. Even the heathen knew that God could and would use His power to fulfill His plan and cause His people to possess the land.

Elijah and Elisha's time

In Elijah and Elisha's day, God's power was once more demonstrated throughout the land as the God of Israel became known as One who answers prayer with signs, wonders and miracles. Once again the course of history was altered by the intervention of God through anointed ministries.

David's time

In David's day God's glory and power were made known in still greater ways. Through great demonstrations of God's power, David and his men defeated the giants in the land and all the enemies that had not been conquered under Joshua's leadership. Truly the reputation of God increased in David's day in a mighty way and men learned that the presence of God in the midst of His people was enough to defeat every enemy.

Solomon's time

In Solomon's day the power of God at work in His people increased still more as the wisdom of God was put on display in Solomon's life. Not only did the wisdom God imparted to Solomon cause him to rule justly among men, but it also provided the setting for forty years of peace in the land.

Jesus and the apostles

In the days of Jesus and the apostles, the preaching of the gospel, accompanied by signs, wonders and miracles, was the ultimate display of God's shining glory. For through the preaching of the gospel, God is able to make Himself known throughout the earth. The most outstanding miracle of those early days is seen in the great multitudes who were touched by God's grace.

Again and again throughout Church history there have been periods of great revival in which multitudes were daily added to the Church. During these times of revival, the kingdom of God has spread throughout the earth until it has been said of men of many generations as it was of the apostles in the early church, "These men (men touched by the presence of God) have turned the world upside down."

The world is waiting for the dawning of a new day. It is waiting for the appearing of an army of believers who so show forth the glory of God that His mighty reputation is made known throughout the earth.

God, Himself, is only waiting for His people to believe the good report of Isaiah: The hand of the Lord is not shortened that he cannot save, and the ear of the Lord is not deaf that He cannot hear, Isaiah 59:1. God is ready to touch us with a fresh anointing, answer our prayers, and pour out His Spirit upon all flesh. Revival will continue so long as God's presence is made known in the lives of His people in clear and tangible demonstrations of His love and power.

Continual Revival

Continual revival is like a continuing rain. First the dry places are made moist, then little streams are formed. As the rain continues, the streams become a river. Finally the river overflows its banks, inundating everything in its path and affecting every living soul by its life-giving presence. The Bible teaches that the kingdom of God will spread and encompass all that is in its path and that it has the potential of spreading throughout the whole earth.

However, just as intermittent rains will never bring a flood that would cover the whole land, so on-and-off revivals will never bring a move of God that will encompass all nations. If the nations of earth are to be reached for Christ and God's plan of world evangelism fulfilled, we must experience continual revival.

Throughout my lifetime the revivals that I have personally seen have been limited in scope and, in general, short-lived. I have always had great difficulty understanding and accepting as normal the nature of these short-lived revivals. We have all seen these kinds of short-lived "revivals" come and go — so much so that most of us believe this is the normal pattern. But it is not. Getting fired up and then cooling off is not God's pattern for a normal Christian life. His pattern is for us to get in the fire and stay there.

Revival fires that go out have the same effect on us as natural fires that go out. We soon lose the warming effect of the fire and begin to cool off. My wife and I have a cabin in the mountains, and if we want to stay warm during the winter we have to keep the fire roaring. So it is in our spiritual lives — we must keep the fire roaring at all times. God wants our churches red-hot. He wants every service cooking and baking with divine glory and power. God wants His glory and power to be demonstrated wall to wall and ceiling to floor.

Furthermore, I have observed that many Christians think of revival only as a time of special meetings and special emphases. But revival is so much more. When we see the overview of God's work of revival in the earth covering centuries, we are able to lift our eyes above our personal or local, on-and-off type experiences of revival.

The Pattern of Revival

When I entered the ministry in the early 1950s, God spoke to me of two truths concerning the great revival that would surface before the eyes of all nations in the closing years of the 20th century. This revival would create such a worldwide response that the impact would continue for years into the next century.

➤ First, I was shown that in my lifetime I would see a much greater display of God's power and glory than my parents saw in their generation.

➤ Second, I was shown that before that revival would come, the Lord would teach His people how revival comes and how to continue the revival from one generation to another. Although our forefathers experienced revival, they were not aware of the order by which revival came and how they could continue in it.

As men of faith come together in unity of the Spirit and share with each other what God is doing in their ministries, I believe that a clear pattern of revival will become evident. The next generation will hold, among their doctrinal beliefs, a well-founded biblical pattern for revival.

If revivals have broken out spontaneously without the aid of the theologians, whose doctrines have until now omitted the all-important biblical declaration on revival, how much greater will the revivals of the future be, as we prepare not only by prayer, but also by doctrine and teaching?

Seldom does God work beyond the scope of our teaching, for He said that the people perish for a lack of knowledge. This generation may gain much hope from Isaiah's prophecy to restore teachers to us, Isaiah 30:20. For as more and more ministries understand and teach the biblical principles of revival, continuing revival will be experienced by more and more people. For our walk generally follows our talk.

I am convinced that the Bible teaches that God's perfect will for His people is to live in a state of continual, never-ending revival. Let us define never-ending revival as the ongoing manifestation of God's glory and power among His people.

Old timers who have seen many revivals come and go are often skeptical when someone talks about the possibility of continual revival. Years of experiencing on-and-off revivals leaves the impression that nothing good lasts and that only in heaven will we continually experience the reality of God's shining presence and open displays of His glory and power.

Jesus taught us to pray:

> *"Thy kingdom come. Thy will be done in earth, as it is in heaven."* Matthew 6:10.

Jesus also said:

> *". . . in heaven . . . angels do always behold the face of my Father . . . ."* Matthew 18:10.

Continual revival, where we upon the earth are always experiencing the manifestation of God's presence, is the answer to Jesus' prayer:

> *"Thy kingdom come. Thy will be done."*

Questions for this chapter on page 199

Christ should not reign as King upon Mount Zion only, because God would cause his power to extend to the remotest regions of the earth.

John Calvin—16th Century

Jesus shall reign where-er the sun doth his successive journeys run.

Isaac Watts — stanza from hymn

No more let sin and sorrow grow, nor thorns infest the ground; He comes to make his blessings flow far as the curse is found...

Isaac Watts — stanza from *Joy to the World*

The fulness of Jesus is not changed, then why are our works so feebly done? Pentecost, is that to be a tradition? The reforming days, are these to be memories only? I see no reason why we should not have a greater Pentecost than Peter saw, and a reformation deeper in its foundations, and truer in its upbuildings than all the reforms which Luther or Calvin achieved.

Charles H. Spurgeon 19th Century

The small and the great, the sane and the insane, the sacred and the profane have been quick to predict when the end might come. They all have one thing in common: They have always been wrong!

Gary DeMar, *Last Day's Madness*

Chapter 4

CHANGING SEASONS

Revival is possible in every generation because God has promised that while the earth remains there will always be times, seasons and new beginnings. Just as we know in the natural that winter will pass, spring will come with its time to plant, followed by the warm days of summer that eventually bring another harvest, so also there are seasons and timings in the spiritual realm. Following times when the world is darkened by sin and the Church is lukewarm, there will always be a new beginning when the Church will be revived and the harvest fields of lost souls will be brought in. Seasons must change in due time, providing for both seedtime and harvest.

God's Covenant with Noah

In Genesis 8:22 God made this promise:

"While the earth remaineth, seedtime and harvest, and cold and heat, and summer and winter, and day and night shall not cease."

This promise was part of the rainbow covenant God gave to Noah and to all generations to follow. Not only did God promise to never again destroy the earth by a flood, but He also promised that the established pattern of changing times and seasons would not cease.

This biblical principle of changing seasons in God's kingdom gives us a hope that goes far beyond anything that man is able to do in his own energy to carry out God's plan as defined in the great commission. For this principle teaches us that God will not limit Himself to man's ability. Should the Church go into a decline and become as cold spiritually as the winter season, we have God's promise that there is still seed in His barn, life in the root of His vine, and hope of a new revival, Haggai 2:19. Yes, spring will come again when the visible signs of life will once more appear throughout the earth.

In the New Testament era, the apostle Paul acknowledged God's eternal covenant of changing seasons by reminding believers of this principle when he told the believers in Thessalonica that they knew the times and seasons perfectly well. See I Thessalonians 5:1. Today, as then, the fact that God deals with His people at appointed times and in changing seasons is an all-important Bible truth.

The changing seasons of seedtime and harvest are divine timings, not human timings. Man must work in harmony with God and plant his seeds in the natural planting time if he is to reap a harvest. The seeds man plants are controlled by a greater principle than human will power or human effort. The seeds will only produce in their season. All of God's times and seasons, whether in the natural or the spiritual, are designed for the benefit, happiness, progress, fruitfulness and prosperity of the human race.

Just as we know in the natural that winter will pass, spring will come with its time to plant, followed by the warm days of summer that eventually bring another harvest, so also there are seasons and timings in the spiritual realm. Following times when the world is darkened by sin and the Church is lukewarm, there will always be a changing of seasons when the Church will be revived and the harvest fields of lost souls will be brought in.

Never say that the days of revival are over. Never say that we will not see another great move of God like we have heard and read about.

Anytime we see the leaves turning brown in autumn and a winter season coming on, we can look beyond those signs to God's promise of changing seasons. We can know that life is still in the root of the plant and that spring will come bringing new life bursting forth on every side. While the earth remains, there will always be times, seasons and new beginnings in both the natural and spiritual kingdoms.

Kingdom Principles

A kingdom is a realm with fixed laws governing everything under its dominion. There are natural kingdoms of plants, animals and man, as well as man-made kingdoms. Then there is the kingdom of God that rules above all other kingdoms. Just as there are laws and principles in all the natural kingdoms of earth, so there are laws and principles controlling everything that transpires in the kingdom of our Lord Jesus Christ. The first law of the kingdom of God is that it has the power to rule over all other kingdoms. Jesus demonstrated this again and again throughout His ministry as He walked on water, turned water into wine, healed the sick, and raised the dead.

The Word of God is like a seed, and it will not return to God until it has accomplished the purpose whereunto He has sent it, Isaiah 55:10,11. This is a law in God's kingdom. The seed must fall into the heart of man and bring forth the work of the Spirit of God in transforming man's nature. Then the Word will return to God through the praises and thanksgiving of those who are exercised unto righteousness by grace, II Corinthians 4:5-15. The seed of God's Word will prosper until the wasteland of human reasoning is restored and the mind of man has become the garden of the Lord.

The laws and principles of God's kingdom will endure to all generations. The times and seasons of God's kingdom will be fulfilled on schedule, whether we are ready or not. Changing of seasons can neither be hurried nor hindered by the will of man, for God has reserved this power unto Himself. See Acts 1:7.

The changing of seasons in God's kingdom is ordained to give the believer the opportunity to sow new seed and prepare for greater harvests. God guarantees that what a man sows that he will also reap. In its season every word will bring forth fruit.

Failure to understand the principle of changing seasons and new beginnings will limit our view of God's work in our lives and in the earth. Without this insight we will often see only the negative conditions around us and hold no hope for revival. We then become locked into an attitude of survival wherein we may feel that our only recourse is to hold on to the end and pray that Jesus will come soon. The idea of surviving the winter season is not bad in itself, but when spring comes a survival attitude becomes the enemy of our future.

Survival mentality

I first became aware of the error of a survival attitude in the late 1960s. I was shocked when God allowed me to see that both my congregation and I were bound with a survival mentality and that all of our efforts were put forth just to survive. He reminded me that those who seek to save their lives will lose them, Luke 17:33.

While it was true that God was working in our midst in spite of our survival attitude, yet the negative thinking of the survival attitude kept us from moving forward with God. We just kept going in circles. Even though we had God's presence and the evidence of His work in our midst, we were still trapped in a survival mentality. Looking back, I can see how His mercy kept us even while we were blinded by the human viewpoint.

God's mercy working in our lives is ordained to draw us into a more positive attitude whereby we will become laborers in the harvest field.

Not understanding God's ways makes it all too easy for us to draw back from God's plan of reaching all the world for Christ and fall into the survival attitude of just staying alive. Anytime we draw back into an attitude of "I must keep myself, or my church, alive," we have forgotten that it is the Holy Spirit who keeps us alive.

Falling into a survival syndrome can easily happen to anyone. Sometimes after a severe trial, people will say, "If trying to go forward produces such intense conflict, I think I would rather find a comfortable, safe place to wait until Jesus comes." Even with a survival attitude we may sometimes be interested in how things are going in other parts of the kingdom, but we usually want to stay far enough from the conflict to avoid getting into the battle. Our attitude is, "Let others take all the chances. As for me and my house, we will just be saved, satisfied, and on our way to heaven." The flaw in that concept is that when we stop going forward, we slide backward. The backward slide is always back into the self-life where the survival attitude is then able to hold us in chains of fear.

One of the greatest dangers of falling into a survival syndrome is that our outlook becomes so negative that we have no faith for revival. When we are blinded by a survival outlook, we will interpret the Scriptures through a negative view based on world conditions and conclude that our only hope for the future is the second coming of Christ. Such an attitude holds little or no hope for the millions of unsaved people in the world. Any doctrine that says there is no hope for millions of earth's people is sadly lacking in the good news of the gospel. Any doctrine that leaves out God's covenant of changing seasons has left out the hope of revival. Noah might have found it easy to slip into a survival way of life, fearing doomsday might be just around the corner, but for the covenant that promised that there would never again be a worldwide flood.

For many years now the free nations of the world have been dominated by a survival mentality. And that which is true of a nation is first true of the Church. A nation, a church or a Christian with a survival attitude is like a person who is sick. For example, when we are ill we do not enjoy life to its fullest, nor are we creative and useful to others. All of our energy is spent in "keeping ourselves alive." However, when we are restored to health and again enjoy the abundant life, our thoughts are no longer on just keeping ourselves alive. We can then move out and again become useful in society.

God Revives the Weary

Our hope of revival depends on God's plan to always revive us when we are weary. Psalm 68:9 says that God sent plentiful rain and confirmed, or revived, the weary congregation. So often it is during the times when the Church is weary that the survival attitude takes over. Just as individual believers do not receive all of God's power in one measure, neither does the Church at large receive the outpouring of the Spirit in one measure; we receive measure by measure. As one wave of revival follows another, the weary Church is restored to its proper place of power and influence.

The pattern in Acts

A study of God's dealings with the first-century Church shows that His plan is to regularly pour out the Spirit and revive His people, keeping His plan of world evangelism always moving onward. The Book of Acts shows the pattern. On the day of Pentecost, the Holy Spirit was poured out in such power that it would seem the disciples had all the spiritual power they would need for the remainder of their lives, Acts 2. Yet Acts 4:29-31 records that the disciples needed to be revived, and so the Spirit of God was poured out upon the believers a second time. This time the outpouring came in such measure that even the building where the disciples were assembled was shaken. Also, to make it clear that times of reviving would be frequent happenings among believers, Peter declared in Acts 3:19 that there would be many times of refreshing from the presence of the Lord. God's promise is clear; there will be times of reviving and refreshing again and again . . . so long as the earth remains.

However, seasons in God's kingdom, unlike natural seasons that change month by month, cannot be confined to a twelve-month calendar. And even though God dealt with Israel in a fifty-year season, or cycle, it was not a hard and fast rule. God is both able and willing to interrupt the cycles and provide a special time of revival whenever it is necessary. God has the power to make wintertime summertime. He makes darkness light. He makes the almond branch to bud while lying before the altar. He gives life where there is death.

Revival in the midst of the years

The prophet Habakkuk, being fully aware that God will sovereignly overrule man's neglect and intervene in man's affairs, called out to the Lord in prayer.

"O Lord, revive thy work in the midst of the years...in wrath remember mercy." Habakkuk 3:2.

The reviving of God's work in the midst of the years is God's act of sovereign intervention to cause the earth to be fruitful and bring forth its increase, establishing the beginning of a new season of sowing and reaping. Thus it has been throughout history that men of faith have heard the Spirit of God saying in their generations, "Forget the former things. Behold, I will do a new thing," Isaiah 43:18,19.

The changing of seasons in God's kingdom is influenced by whether the Church is walking in the Spirit or the flesh. A time of spiritual lethargy can be compared to a winter season in the natural. When unfavorable conditions prevent harvest time, God will sovereignly intervene, guaranteeing that there will always be a revival harvest time in every generation.

Habakkuk could pray for God to revive His work in the midst of the years because he was listening to the voice of the Lord. He was not listening to the many earthly voices that could only see the future through a negative human viewpoint. Habakkuk was listening to God — our God of redemption and mercy. Habakkuk had heard a word from the Lord that gave him hope. He understood that the solutions to the problems in his nation would not come through men's wisdom or strength. He understood that just as God had revived His work in years past, so the nation would again be delivered from the evil conditions of that time. Habakkuk understood that God would make known His mercy in times of wrath. *Times of wrath* are another way of describing winter seasons — times when natural conditions seem to say there is little or no hope for a great harvest of souls. Revival is the time when mercy rejoices over wrath and becomes the rule of the day.

Throughout both Bible history and the Church age, God has made His mercy known in the earth. In the time of Moses, when cruel oppression was upon the children of Israel, God made Himself known to the great Pharaoh of Egypt as the time changed in favor of God's people. The children of Israel did not expect it. Pharaoh did not expect it. But it was time for a change, and the change came in a miraculous way as God intervened on behalf of His people and kept His plan on schedule. See Exodus 14.

The changing of times will ultimately come to every generation. Either the saints of God will press into the things of the Spirit and grow up into Christ to a level of maturity sufficient to release a wave of revival, or God will sovereignly step in and send revival Himself. In either case those who are seeking God and who are preparing for revival will not be disappointed.

Eli and Samuel

Another example of changing times where God revived His work in the midst of the years is recorded in I Samuel, Chapters 2-4. In those days the glory of the Lord had departed from the house of the Lord. Eli, the priest, was blind to the timings and plan of God. He had grown fat with self-satisfaction and was unable to restrain evil in his generation. Yet, lest the light of God should go out, God called for the beginning of a new season. The child Samuel was chosen by God to be the instrument for a new work in a new season. This was God's way to guarantee another time of revival and restoration in Israel.

King Hezekiah

Changing times were also evident in the life and reign of King Hezekiah. See II Chronicles 29. Hezekiah came into leadership during a time when Israel was desolate. At that time the house of the Lord was in disrepair, the glory of the Lord had departed, and the sacrifices were no longer offered. But times changed, and under a new administration Hezekiah began to restore the house of the Lord. He restored the altars, the pillars, the priests, the royal and holy garments, and the offerings and sacrifices. As the sacrifices were offered again, the song of the Lord began, signaling the beginning of another springtime in the kingdom of God.

> *"For, lo, the winter is past, the rain is over and gone; the flowers appear on the earth; the time of the singing of the birds is come, and the voice of the turtle is heard in our land."* Song of Solomon 2:11,12.

The prophecies of Daniel teach us that changing times not only effect things in the kingdom of God but also in all other kingdoms of earth. In the Book of Daniel, we see how each time God's hand came on His people and times were changed, there was also a changing and shaking that took place in the natural kingdoms.

King Nebuchadnezzar's dream of the great image is a perfect example of how God's power at work in His kingdom effects all other kingdoms. Nebuchadnezzar not only saw all earthly kingdoms symbolized in the dream of the great image, but he saw a stone that was cut out without hands which broke the great image into pieces and then became a great mountain and filled the whole earth, Daniel 2:31-35,44. Daniel interpreted this dream for the king, telling him that the four parts of the great image represented different earthly kingdoms, including Babylon. He also said that the stone that broke the earthly kingdoms into pieces represented the power of God's kingdom at work in the earth to overcome the world system and bring in the harvest of souls from among the nations.

Never will God's plan for His kingdom change. Never will the powers of His kingdom be limited. Never will God be satisfied with anything less than the best in His kingdom. The kingdom of God will ultimately be manifested among the nations in the total fulfillment of all things spoken by the mouth of the holy prophets since the world began, Acts 3:21.

Since the time of Daniel, many kingdoms of men have come and gone but the kingdom of God has remained. From generation to generation, the Holy Spirit has stirred and revived believers in one way or another so that God's kingdom has continued to be a major force among the nations.

New Season of Opportunity

Today the Church has come to a new season of opportunities. We are being called at this changing of times to arise and move out beyond our borders, to go beyond our past experiences, and to live beyond the memories of what has been. We are being called to arise and move into a greater vision. Jesus is calling for us to press on, and He is increasing the work of His Spirit at every level of the kingdom. Faith is reaching an all-time high. Hope for the greatest revival in history is appearing everywhere. Millions of people around the world are sensing a shaking and are experiencing an awakening; they are asking, "Can this be true? Can this be God? Can this be the beginning of new and greater ministries than we have ever known?"

Yes. This is a time of changing seasons. If you feel a stirring and an awakening in your spirit, let me assure you that this is not a temporary stirring. This is the beginning of new timings that will continue for years.

We are moving into a new season. We may call it a new era, a new age, or a new day. The fact that it is happening is the greater fact; how we may define it is secondary. The important thing is that the sun has set on that which was in the past and has risen on a new day of glory. Our eyes have not seen nor our ears heard the things the Holy Spirit is now beginning to reveal to our generation. Get ready to believe God for greater things than we have ever dared hope for in the past.

God is moving by His Spirit. He is telling His people that it is the changing of times. No more will we say that things will be as they have always been, but we will now say that things will be as God has promised. Times are changing and a new season has come! A new time of reviving and restoration has come upon the Church.

Earthly kings and kingdoms of our day will bow before the kingdom of God just as King Nebuchadnezzar bowed in his day. Leaders of nations will fall at the feet of Jesus and declare that He is ruler over all nations. Those who rule over the great kingdoms of financial and natural resources will bow at the feet of Jesus. Shame will come upon the kingdoms of this earth and their leaders who have resisted all that is decent and moral. Divine confrontation is coming, and those who have brought this nation to the brink of destruction will be ashamed to show their faces in public. See Isaiah 14.

While it appears that the Church has been losing the battle against sin and immorality, we have actually been turning the other cheek and waiting in quiet confidence for the Lord to arise and fight for us. Something wonderful has been happening through the years as we have waited for the Lord to arise and bring about a changing of times. While the world has seen the Church in her weakness, turning the other cheek, apparently unable and unwilling to fight back, Jesus has been revealing Himself afresh to His people preparing us for a new visitation and revival.

In the changing of times, God is not limited to one brief display of His power and glory; He will reveal Himself again and again. He will multiply the blessing until it becomes so great that it is pressed down, shaken together and running over. These multiplied blessings come because it is the time of harvest. For years the good seed of God's Word has been sown throughout the earth, and it is now time to reap.

One great harvest has already been reaped in the early part of this century. The middle years of this century have been a preparation for another harvest as the seed has been sown by every means possible, from the simple gospel tract to the worldwide gospel television ministries. The hearts of millions have been prepared. Now we shall reap as never in history.

Questions for this chapter on page 201

Praise is a soul in flower.

Thomas Watson, 17th Century Puritan

Praise shall conclude that work which prayer began.

William Jenkyn, 17th Century Puritan

The servants of the Lord are to sing His praise in this life to the world's end; and in the next life, world without end.

John Boys

Self-love may lead us to prayer, but love to God excites us to praises.

Thomas Manton, 17th Century Puritan

Chapter 5

REVIVAL IN THE YEAR OF JUBILEE

J ubilee in many ways is the Old Testament equivalent of what we have come to know in New Testament times as revival. In the times and seasons of God's dealings with Israel, He established a fifty-year cycle and appointed that in the fiftieth year every man's full inheritance would be restored. The fiftieth year was called the year of jubilee. See Leviticus 25.

Just as jubilee for natural Israel was a time of coming back into full possession of their inheritance, so times of revival for the Church are times of coming into a full possession of our inheritance in Christ. Everything that jubilee promises, revival is.

Jesus, Himself, brought the anointing of the year of jubilee right out of the Old Testament and made it an integral part of the New Testament Church when He said,

> *"The Spirit of the Lord is upon me...to proclaim the acceptable year of the Lord."* Luke 4:18,19.

Jesus was acting out His role as the Lion of the tribe of Judah, spokesman of the house of praise, as He proclaimed the year of jubilee in preaching deliverance to the captives. Later, the apostle Paul wrote in II Corinthians 6:2 of the acceptable time. Both Paul and Jesus were showing us that the effects of the year of jubilee are fulfilled in believers in the Church age.

Jubilee in both the Old and New Testaments is a time when God's power liberates man, restoring to him his full inheritance as promised in God's Word. What Israel experienced only during the twelve months of the year of jubilee in the Old Testament, we in the New Testament may experience every day throughout our entire Christian lives when revival fires are burning in our hearts.

Jubilee

The word *jubilee* means "the blended sound of trumpets proclaiming liberty throughout the land." The official release of jubilee to set all the captives free and bring restoration began with the sounding of the trumpets. The blowing of the trumpets was first the exclusive privilege of a few priests in the Levitical system. But later, in the tabernacle of David, a new order was established that included all who praised. The psalmist was inspired by the Holy Spirit to declare that the *horns,* or trumpets, of the Lord were the praises of all His people. Psalm 148:14. Therefore, the jubilee decree was lifted from its natural setting and placed in a spiritual setting. In the spiritual setting, all believers are encouraged to praise the Lord.

Praise

"Let everything that hath breath [the spirit] *praise the Lord....*" Psalm 150:6.

From the time of David's teaching on spiritual sacrifices and the order of worship practiced in the tabernacle of David until now, God's power has been released through the praises of His people in setting the captives free in the same manner as He responded to the sounding of the trumpets. Where there are people praising the Lord, there God will be setting men free.

Psalm 67 shows us that praise is a key Bible principle leading to revival.

"...Let the people praise thee, O God; let all the people praise thee. Then shall the earth yield her increase; and God, even our own God, shall bless us...." Psalm 67:5,6.

Times of revival are always times of increase in the kingdom of God.

As we see how the trumpets, or praises, of jubilee are instrumental in releasing the power of God to intervene in the affairs of men, we will see how jubilee and revival are terms that express the same work of God in men's lives.

The jubilee teaching is like a diamond with many facets. It is a blending together of every promise of God provided to set man free from all bondages. As our praises rise to God, His power flows out to the nations.

- ➤ Jubilee is a restoring of liberty to the captives; so is revival.

- ➤ Jubilee is a release from bondage and a forgiveness of debts and sins; so is revival.

- ➤ Jubilee is a returning to the land of one's inheritance; so is revival.

- ➤ Jubilee is a restoration of all that has been lost; again, so is revival.

- ➤ Jubilee is a restoration of complete fellowship between God and man; this truly is revival!

Praise brings victory

From the beginning, God has ordained praise as a key principle to a life of daily abundance for His people. Adam and Eve freely praised and worshiped God day after day in the garden of Eden. They walked in His presence in the cool of the day as the Holy Spirit moved in their midst. Since that time God has worked in the hearts of men throughout the ages to regain the special fellowship found only in praise.

As a part of this continuing work, God led David to establish the way of praise as the everyday way of life for His people. As they daily, around the clock, praised the Lord, it was as though the trumpets of jubilee were sounding continually. This daily jubilee, or revival power, released the armies of Israel into the realm of the supernatural, enabling them to defeat all their enemies and bring complete peace in all their borders. The psalmist testified that praise not only brought them jubilee in the courts of the Lord, but also brought them victory on the battlefield, as he wrote, in Psalm 149, that with the two-edged sword in their hands and the high praises of God in their mouths they were able to tread down the wicked, execute the judgments written, and subdue the kingdoms of this world.

This was not the only time in the history of God's people when praise became the means of releasing the supernatural power of God, giving the people victory over their adversaries. In Joshua's day the walls of Jericho fell down flat at the sound of the trumpets and the shouts of the people, Joshua 6:20. In King Jehoshaphat's day the singers were appointed to go before the army of Judah. As they sang and praised the Lord, God sent ambushments and the enemy destroyed themselves, II Chronicles 20:21-25.

Praise is as the sound of the trumpets announcing the entrance of the King into His sanctuary. At the same time, praise is also the sound of the trumpets releasing the King to go forth in supernatural power before the army and fight the battle and secure the victory.

Proclamation of liberty

Praise is not designed to be just a mood conditioner whereby we lift our spirits by singing songs and hymns. While praise does lift our spirits in times of conflict when the enemy intrudes into our land and tries to rob us of our inheritance, praise also is the proclamation of liberty from all destructive forces and the acknowledgment that God will arise and through His supernatural power fight for us in the time of battle. Not only is God's presence manifested to believers in a special way through praise, but it is also manifested forth into the battlefield.

> "And the sons of Aaron, the priests, shall blow with the trumpets; and they shall be to you for an ordinance for ever throughout your generations. And if ye go to war in your land against the enemy that oppresseth you, then ye shall blow an alarm with the trumpets; and ye shall be remembered before the Lord your God, and ye shall be saved from your enemies," Numbers 10:8,9.

"God is gone up with a shout, the Lord with the sound of a trumpet," Psalm 47:5.

"Let God arise, let His enemies be scattered...," Psalm 68:1.

When we praise the Lord, our praises are as the sounding of the trumpets that causes the Lord to arise and do battle.

God has ordained that through our praise He will arise from the mercy seat and enforce the jubilee decree, sending forth rays of light and power among His people. These rays are expressions of the power of His presence that, according to Malachi 4 brings healing to the land. The psalmist prayed that the Lord would send forth the rays of His light and power when he said:

"...O Shepherd of Israel...thou that dwellest between the cherubim, shine forth....Turn us again [revive, or restore, us], *O God, and cause your face to shine* [upon us]; *and we shall be saved* [delivered from our bondages and made free from the oppression of the enemy, giving us the victory]," Psalm 80:1-3.

Divine light and power

In Psalm 18 David used several symbolic terms which are key words describing the rays of divine light and power that shine forth when God arises from the throne to scatter His enemies. David spoke of God's power as thunder, bolts of lightning, and coals of fire. A study of the scriptures dealing with these symbolic expressions of God's power reveals that the *thunder* represents the voice of God giving the command, the *lightning* represents the power of the Holy Spirit, and the *coals of fire* represent the spoken word of faith, which is a *rhema* word of God. The thunder, lightning, and coals of fire are God's instruments of war by which He scatters His enemies.

Daniel 7:9,10 describes the scene around the throne when believers are praising and tells of God's power issuing forth from before Him as fiery streams bringing revival and jubilee.

One of the greatest examples of jubilee in Scripture is the restoration of Israel after seventy years of exile in Babylon. This example also illustrates the spiritual application to the jubilee truth, for Israel's deliverance was not during the fiftieth year of their calendar. God overruled the 50 year cycle as He intervened and gave Israel a jubilee by the higher principle of spiritual laws pertaining to the new order of God's kingdom.

The Kingdom of God

During the time God was preparing to deliver Israel from bondage in Babylon, spiritual principles were introduced showing that the kingdom of God operates among all nations and not just when Israel is in the promised land.

God revealed through Daniel's prophecies that whereas the kingdom of God had previously existed only in the nation Israel, it would now be set up among all nations. We read in Daniel 2:44,45 that God's kingdom is like a great stone cut out of the mountain that will roll throughout the earth and crush all other kingdoms.

> *"And the kingdom and dominion, and the greatness of the kingdom under the whole heaven, shall be given to the people of the saints of the Most High, whose kingdom is an everlasting kingdom, and all dominions* [all other kingdoms] *shall serve and obey Him."* Daniel 7:27.

The next verse then declares that the spreading of the kingdom throughout the whole earth is the end of Daniel's vision.

> *"Hitherto is the end of the matter. As for me Daniel, my thoughts much troubled me, and my countenance changed in me: but I kept the matter in my heart."* Daniel 7:28.

At this point we must perceive that Israel does not have exclusive rights to the kingdom of God, for Jesus said,

> *"And this gospel of the kingdom shall be preached in all the world for a witness unto all nations; and then shall the end come."* Matthew 24:14.

Furthermore, the kingdom of God does not exist in a natural realm but in a supernatural dimension.

By the time Israel came out of exile from Babylon, they had come to understand that the supernatural laws of the kingdom of God would work in them no matter where they were, freeing them from their fears and bondage. Therefore they were able to return with singing, dancing and great joy, just as Jeremiah had prophesied. See Jeremiah 31:10-12. The return of Israel from Babylon is a great example of how revival works among the nations to set the captives free.

The gospel of the kingdom must be preached

Jesus said that His kingdom is not of this world and that except we be born again we cannot even see the kingdom of God. John 18:36; 3:3-5.

The disciples asked Jesus, in Acts 1:6, if He would restore the kingdom to Israel at that time. We must now ask a further question. Does the disciples' question imply the idea that someday the kingdom would be the exclusive possession of Israel? No, it does not.

Jesus had already said in Matthew 24 that this gospel of the kingdom of God must be preached to all nations. Therefore the appropriate answer to their question is found in Acts 1:7, where Jesus said that the Father has reserved in His own power the times of restoration of the kingdom, which are times of revival in the Church throughout the nations. Then Jesus went one step further and told how the Father would restore the kingdom. He said, in verse 8, that they would receive power that would make them witnesses unto Jesus unto the uttermost parts of the earth. The Book of Revelation declares that the kingdoms of this world have become the kingdoms of our God and of His Christ, Revelation 11:15.

God's Kingdom among all nations

Daniel was the first of the prophets to understand that the kingdom of God would be set up among all the nations, and revival and jubilee would be experienced by men of all generations to come. Daniel personally experienced the effective working of the higher spiritual laws of God's kingdom during the time of the kingdom of Babylon and the kingdom of the Medes and Persians. Daniel discovered that true worshipers gather around the throne of God in the heavenlies in a spiritual dimension. Though the temple in Jerusalem lay in ruins, still Daniel saw multitudes gathered around the throne. He beheld the Ancient of Days opening the books and saw that the time had come for the saints of the Most High God to possess the kingdom throughout the whole earth, Daniel 7.

Outpouring of the Holy Spirit

Revival is a supernatural work in the Spirit in each man's heart. Through revival God causes the supernatural laws of the kingdom to overrule the desolate state of man's natural condition, bringing a release in the spirit so that even the most desperate individual can become a new creature.

Praise not only brings an inner working of God's presence in each believer and an outward release of God's power in the battlefield but praise produces that vast dimension in the work of jubilee for which we so yearn in our day. Our praises, individually and collectively, are like the vapors drawn by the sun into the atmosphere, forming clouds to pour out rain upon the earth.

God is preparing His people everywhere to praise Him more and more as he brings the Church ever nearer to a great and mighty harvest. The more we praise Him the more the vapors of spiritual power ascend from the tabernacle of the Lord and form the clouds that bring the rains of revival, Job 36:27-29.

The rain of the Spirit

We read in Psalm 68 how praise releases the rain that comes down to revive the weary congregation. The rain of the Spirit that comes to revive does not just come to keep us alive, but it comes as the early rain to cause the seed to grow and as the latter rain to cause the fields to ripen unto harvest.

Joel says that God will give us the former and latter rain in the first month. This is truly a perfect description of jubilee and revival. During times of mighty revivals, when the Church reaches peak performance, there is no more saying, *"There are yet four months, and then cometh the harvest."* John 4:35. For the same month that the early rain gives growth to the seed, the latter rain will come to bring the harvest. Joel 2:23. This speaks of a supernatural harvest and a true revival — many of which have transpired throughout history. These times of supernatural harvest are described in Amos 9:13,14:

> *"Behold, the days come, saith the Lord, that the plowman shall overtake the reaper, and the treader of grapes him that soweth seed; and the mountains shall drop sweet wine, and all the hills shall melt.*
> *And I will bring again the captivity of my people of Israel, and they shall build the waste cities, and inhabit them; and they shall plant vineyards, and drink the wine thereof; they shall also make gardens, and eat the fruit of them."*

Joel 2 teaches us that the rain speaks symbolically of the outpouring of the Spirit. The prophet foresaw that the Spirit would be poured out on all flesh and not just in the nation Israel. Thus we see that through the work of jubilee and revival the supernatural kingdom of God is made known among all nations.

As we see praise and worship being restored to churches throughout the world, we can all find great hope. The restoring of true praise is a key sign that a new wave of revival is coming upon God's people. Praise and jubilee go hand in hand. Praise and revival go hand in hand. Believers in any nation and in any generation can experience revival in such a measure that all the enemies of God and the Church will be put to flight when the churches are restored to true praise and worship.

Rejoice in the Lord always

We will experience a deepening in the flow of revival as we learn to follow the scriptures that teach us to rejoice in the Lord always and to give thanks in everything. Praise is the power that releases the rain of the Spirit from the heavenly clouds of glory. The rain, in turn, is the power that releases the increase of the earth. The more we praise

God, from whom all blessings flow, the more we will experience the restoring, reviving benefits of jubilee.

Jeremiah 34:15-17 agrees with Joel 2, establishing that the work of jubilee is fulfilled in the outpouring of the Spirit upon all flesh. The prophet said that everyone was to proclaim liberty upon his brother and his neighbor. As we said earlier in this chapter, jubilee means "the blended sound of trumpets proclaiming liberty throughout the land." Our praises are as the sounding of trumpets for the deliverance of others. A praising individual is an encouragement to everyone around him. A praising congregation of believers releases liberty upon everyone in their midst.

Our praising does far more to deliver the captives than pointing fingers of accusation and pressuring people to change their lifestyles. Accusation and pressure always draw negative human responses. But giving God thanks for His promise to deliver the captives and praising Him in advance for His faithfulness to do what He says He will do always draws a positive and supernatural response from the Almighty.

Released in praise

Luke 13 gives us an example of what happens when God releases just one person in praise. Jesus came into a church where nobody was praising the Lord. He found a woman there who had been unable to lift herself up for eighteen years. I see this woman as a picture of people who cannot praise, for the psalmist said that praise was like the lifting up of the heads, or gates, and the lifting up and opening of the everlasting doors, Psalm 24. When Jesus loosed her, not only did she begin to praise the Lord but the text says that all the people began to rejoice for all the wonderful works that Christ had done. And the ruler of the synagogue who had kept the people in bondage for so long was silenced.

If it happened then, it can happen in our time. God's promise to send revival is for all men in all generations, Psalm 100:5.

As we continue to praise God, we will be lifted from the low places of confusion and from the ruts and prisons of religious traditions that have diluted and even denied the power of God. God will lift us into the heavenlies where light is pure, truth is understandable, and knowledge is workable. Knowledge will become more than empty theory. Such knowledge of the Lord will make lasting impressions on us. We will then experience changes in our attitudes and our relationships with others as we are conformed to God's highest level of love.

Questions for this chapter on page 203

The covenant concept of "all nations blessed" comes to the fore in the poetry of the Psalter. The composers of the Book of Praise of the Old Testament looked for the triumph of the church upon earth. . . One of the contributing factors to the present day pessimism, gloominess, defeatism within the church is the omitting of the Psalms from the hymn books. They should have first place. The best musical talent of the church should be occupied in setting the Psalms to fitting music.

J. Marcellus Kik, *An Eschatology of Victory*

They who from hence urge the use of music in religious worship must, by the same rule, introduce dancing, for they went together, as in David's dancing before the ark . . .

Matthew Henry, English Puritan

You always get, as the chief characteristic in very revival, a great spirit of rejoicing and of singing. Singing generally is a part of a revival—not a worked up singing, but a spontaneous bursting forth into song.

D. Martyn Lloyd-Jones, *Joy Unspeakable—Power and Renewal in the Holy Spirit*

GOD'S GLORY IN THE CHURCH AGAIN

Revival is always the result of God's manifested glory and is the miracle of miracles. Revival is the miraculous result in men's hearts of God's manifested glory before their eyes.

God's Manifested Presence

When the Bible speaks of the glory of the Lord, it is speaking of God's manifested presence. God's manifested presence is easily recognized by man because it is a supernatural work of the Spirit of God.

Moses saw God's glory (manifested presence) in the burning bush and on the mountaintop. The children of Israel and the Egyptians were eyewitnesses to God's glory when, through many miracles, God's people were delivered from Egypt. In Solomon's day the temple was filled with God's glory in the form of a visible cloud. In Jesus' day the people witnessed the glory of God through demonstrations of Jesus' supernatural power over natural elements and substances, and through His power over disease, demons and death. Paul saw God's glory on the road to Damascus, and his ministry was a constant display of God's supernatural powers to the people of many nations. The apostles and the early Church saw God's glory in the gifts of the Spirit and the miracles that happened when they prayed in Jesus' name. We should expect similar manifestations of God's glory in our day.

The God of the supernatural

The more we see God as the God of the supernatural, the easier it is for us to believe in revival. When natural things are touched by the supernatural, they testify of God's mighty power thereby showing that no natural circumstance is final.

We are more aware of the supernatural work and power of God's presence during times of praise and worship than at any other times. It is as though our praises turn on a supernatural power switch which causes the room to be flooded with a supernatural demonstration of God's presence.

Supernatural demonstrations of God's presence are detected in different ways by different people. Some will immediately recognize the glory of the Lord as it is manifested during times of worship and will say, "This is God's presence." Others, not knowing that God's glory is being demonstrated will nevertheless sense a brightening of attitude, a lifting of burdens, and even a reviving from physical weariness — all of which are a result of the supernatural touching the natural, leaving a deposit of the Divine Life upon the person who has received the blessing. Repeated encounters of this nature will cause most people to become aware that the refreshing experience of praise is more than a natural phenomenon; it is a definite touch of God upon them in a tangible and meaningful way.

Just as electricity is not visible as it flows through the conduits that carry it into our homes, but must be manifested through a light fixture, so it is with the glory of the Lord. The supernatural power of God is always available through every covenant, promise and word of Scripture, but it is not discernible until there is a fixture or outlet through which it can be displayed. Both electricity and the glory of

God must have a receptacle to receive and manifest their power and energy. Just as a light bulb must have an intact inner filament and be screwed into an outlet to which power is turned on for electricity to be manifested, so believers must have a faith (a heart and mind to receive God's promises) that is intact, be screwed in tightly to God's truth, and be turned on to praise if they are to release manifestations of God's glory and the supernatural.

Gathering of praisers

Although we can experience God's manifested presence in times of private worship and prayer, it is as a rain shower compared to the deluge we can experience when many praisers and worshipers are gathered together. Even as clouds have to form again and again to release electrical energy in the form of lightning, so God's people must gather regularly for praise and worship to create the atmosphere for the glory of the Lord to be demonstrated.

Years ago, as I began to understand the connection between praise and manifestations of God's glory, I realized that the Lord would have to do a new thing to raise up churches that would praise Him in every service until His glory was evident and the supernatural was restored on a regular basis among His people. As I inquired of the Lord if such a thing were possible, He began to show me through many scriptures the new thing that He would do in my lifetime.

Reviving the Waste Places

Isaiah 61:4 shows us that the new thing is the reviving of old waste places and the restoring of the good things that were understood by former generations.

> *"Behold, I will do a new thing... I will even make a way in the wilderness, and the rivers in the desert...I will give drink to my people, my chosen. This people have I formed for myself, they shall show forth my praise,"* Isaiah 43:19-21.

I understood from these scriptures and others that the people through whom God would work to restore the old waste places and revive the wilderness, making it a watered garden, would be a people of praise and worship. And I began to see that wherever we see praise being restored, we will see revival breaking forth.

David the praiser

One of the best Bible examples of the power of praise to bring revival and healing to the land is that of King David. David understood that God's presence was manifested in a special way in praise. He wrote:

> *"Yet thou art holy, O thou who art enthroned upon the praises of Israel,"* Psalm 22:3, NAS.

David was led by the Holy Spirit to establish a new order of tabernacle worship in which praise became the sacrifice that was offered unto the Lord instead of the bodies of animals. David wrote:

> *"O Lord, open thou my lips; and my mouth shall show forth thy praise. For thou desirest not sacrifice* [animal bodies]; *else would I give it: thou delightest not in burnt offering* [of animal bodies]," Psalm 51:15,16.

The bodies of the animals offered in the morning and evening daily sacrifices were types of our praises, which Hosea referred to as the "calves" or the sacrifices of our lips. Hosea 14:2. Jeremiah also spoke of the sacrifice of praise:

> *"...bring the sacrifice of praise into the house of the Lord...,"* Jeremiah 33:11.

In retrospect, we could say that just as David spoke prophetically of the atonement of Christ in many of the psalms, so he also instituted a new order of worship that was a prophetic enactment of the New Testament order. In the New Testament order, there are no animal sacrifices; the only blood sacrifice required has been provided in the atonement of Jesus Christ.

Praise has great bearing on revival in our time. Praise not only releases God's power to flow out of our hearts and bring the blessing of revival to others, but praise also manifests God's presence to the individual believer. The sacrifices of praise remove the fleshly veils of the mind. The Holy Spirit is then able to do a complete work of renewal in the heart of man. Hebrews 10 teaches us that by His crucifixion Jesus opened the veil that separated man from God's presence.

> *"By him therefore let us offer the sacrifice of praise to God continually, that is, the fruit of our lips giving thanks to his name,"* Hebrews 13:15.

Singing songs and praising God is a very normal experience for any believer. Yet it is during such times when God's glory is recognized most.

God's desire has always been to dwell with man in a very personal way. Confining God's presence behind the veil in the holy of holies was not satisfactory. Thus, in His death, Jesus not only rent the veil of the temple, but He rent the veil of the flesh, making it possible for those who worship the Father through Jesus Christ to have access to God. God, foreseeing the work of Christ in opening the veil, revealed as far back as King David that true worshipers would prepare God a habitation of praise so that He might dwell with every believer in a personal way.

The sanctuary is the place the Lord has ordained and created where God and man come together in harmony, where the heavenly and the earthly are so perfectly blended that there is no enmity. It is the place where God's grace is fully experienced in man's heart.

The order of praise and worship

During David's day praise and worship as described and taught in the Psalms became the established order by which the people came into God's presence. These sacrifices of praise and worship included lifting up of the hands, singing, shouting, clapping, dancing, playing musical instruments, bowing down, and lying prostrate before the Lord.

We learn from David's example that these many expressions of worship can be offered in spontaneous inspiration in praise, as David did when he danced and sang when the ark was brought to the city of God.

We also learn that praise can be offered in a skillful, orderly fashion. This often takes the form of an orderly processional. Psalm 68 speaks of the *goings* of God the King in the sanctuary. In Psalm

77:13 these *goings* of God are called *the way of the Lord in the sanctuary*. The Hebrew meanings behind the words *goings* and *ways* and the phrase *the way of the Lord in the sanctuary* speak to us of the order and procedures that we are directed to follow in times of worship. When these procedures are followed in an orderly fashion it becomes the processional which ushers God's presence into the sanctuary as He ascends to be enthroned in the praises of His people. Praise enthrones God.

Psalm 68:25 spells out the order of the procedure of praise in the sanctuary. First come the singers. The singing of psalms, hymns and spiritual songs, with grace and melody in our hearts, must be the dominating factor in praise and worship. See Ephesians 5:19. The singers are followed by the players of instruments. Instruments are to be a part of worship but not the dominating part; the instruments are to carry a supporting role and gently blend with the voices and lift them into higher realms of praise. After that are the dancers with the tambourines. Exodus 15 first records that groups of women danced and praised the Lord with tambourines. The groups of dancing women were a normal part of Israel's frequent celebrations, both on their feast days and in celebration of great victories.

These many expressions of praise and worship serve various purposes. Some are symbolic of our surrender to God and our obedience to Him. Others symbolize our joy, our zeal, and our acknowledgment of approaching victory. Praising the Lord in the dance has so many Bible purposes that it is almost a subject unto itself.

Praise from the heart

However, Isaiah warns us against praising with our lips only, when our heart is not in it. Praise void of a heart-felt love becomes only empty ritual. True praise is more than words, sounds and gestures. True praise presupposes many factors. Praise and worship acknowledge God's all-sufficient gift of His son, Jesus, and the many provisions that are ours in Christ. We praise God for who He is, for His goodness and mercy, and for all that He has done for us. Our praises are full of Him. He is enthroned in them. God is not enthroned in our good works or our efforts to serve Him in the flesh. He is enthroned in praise. When we praise God, we acknowledge that of ourselves we can do nothing, even as we acknowledge that He has already done everything that is required or needed for our salvation and spiritual life.

So we see that although David was a praiser and he set up an order of worship that included continual praise, there was the knowing and the appreciating of all that God is and all that He has provided incorporated in David's praise. Praise was not a ritual to David; praise came out of a life totally yielded to God. The psalmist was speaking from this position of knowing, following and appreciating God when he wrote of the importance to praise more and more.

> *"Every day will I bless thee; and I will praise thy name forever and ever."* Psalm 145:2.

> *"Seven times a day do I praise thee...."* Psalm 119:164.

> *"At midnight I will rise to give thanks...."* Psalm 119:62.

> *"From the rising of the sun unto the going down of the same the Lord's name is to be praised."* Psalm 113:3.

> *"Bless ye the Lord, all ye servants of the Lord, which by night stand in the house of the Lord. Lift up your hands in the sanctuary, and bless the Lord."* Psalm 134:1,2.

Forty years of peace

David appointed praisers to minister to the Lord in shifts, twenty-four hours a day. Thus the place of worship that David set up on Mount Zion was continually filled with praise. And since God dwells in the praise of His people, the people of that day experienced revival.

As a result David and his mighty men were able to accomplish greater feats than all their forefathers. They utterly destroyed all their enemies and stopped war in all their borders. They took possession of more of the promised land than at any other time. They ushered in a forty-year period of peace that continued throughout Solomon's lifetime. Historians have referred to this time as the "Golden Age of Israel."

Revival in David's day

The revival that began in David's day was ongoing and ever-increasing. When Solomon came to the throne of Israel, he followed the ways of his father David, and his generation continued to offer sacrifices of praise and worship according to the order of David. God was enthroned in those praises, and His presence and supernatural abilities continued to give Israel victory and revival.

The revival died out towards the end of Solomon's life because he did not practice in his family life the order of God that he had learned from his father David. This again illustrates that going through the motions of praise in church is not enough. Our hearts must be right with God and our lives must be right with each other for praise to be a vehicle of revival.

Like Solomon's son, Rehoboam, many other kings also did not walk in the ways of their father David. During times that Israel departed from a true and sincere worship of God, the spiritual life of Israel slipped lower and lower, and many did wickedly in the sight of the Lord. God, in His mercy, often intervened and raised up a restorer who reestablished the practice of praise and worship as it was in David's day. Always when men's hearts were made right with God and the order of worship which David taught was followed, the glory of God returned and the spiritual life of Israel rose accordingly.

Key to Revival

As the prophet Isaiah sought revival in his time, he discovered that David's order of worship was not only the key to revival in David's day but in all generations that should follow. He wrote:

> *"...I will make an everlasting covenant with you, even the sure mercies of David, whom I have given you for a witness, a leader and a commander,"* Isaiah 55:3,4.

From David's time until now, God's work of revival has always been to restore an open revelation of His presence to man on an individual basis.

The apostle Paul left no doubt as to the place and purpose of praise in the New Testament Church as he wrote:

"By him [the resurrected Jesus] *therefore let us offer the sacrifice of praise to God continually, that is, the fruit of our lips giving thanks to His name,"* Hebrews 13:15.

Praise continually

Please notice that Paul went so far as to say that this offering of praise should be made continually. Being even more explicit, Paul wrote:

"Speaking to yourselves in psalms and hymns and spiritual songs, singing and making melody in your heart to the Lord," Ephesians 5:19.

"Let the word of Christ dwell in you richly in all wisdom; teaching and admonishing one another in psalms and hymns and spiritual songs, singing with grace in your hearts to the Lord," Colossians 3:16.

"How is it then, brethren? when ye come together, every one of you hath a psalm, hath a doctrine, hath a tongue, hath a revelation, hath an interpretation. Let all things be done unto edifying," I Corinthians 14:26.

Not only did Paul speak of praising and worshiping according to the order in Psalms (David's order), but so did the apostle James. James spoke of God's promise to restore the order of worship in the tabernacle-of-David era as he quoted from the prophet Amos:

"After this I will return, and will build again the tabernacle of David, which is fallen down; and I will build again the ruins thereof, and I will set it up: that the residue of men might seek after the Lord, and all the Gentiles, upon whom my name is called, saith the Lord, who doeth all these things. Known unto God are all his works from the beginning of the world," Acts 15:16-18.

Tabernacle of David

In the tabernacle-of-David style of worship, we acknowledge, through our sacrifice of praise, God's all-sufficient gift of salvation and its accompanying provisions. When we lose the awareness of His free gift of grace and mercy, we go back to trying to bring God an offering of our human efforts seeking to earn His favor and seeking to bring us into His presence through our own good works. The sacrifice of praise is an acknowledgment of God's total provision, grace and power.

No form of praising God is of any value when the heart is not involved. No form of praise glorifies God unless it comes directly out of a heart of thankfulness, for God's goodness and provisions.

Throughout history many have found it all too easy to lose their awareness and appreciation of God's grace, mercy and total provision. During the Dark Ages, the awareness of God's free gift of grace was lost, along with the order of praise and worship according to the Psalms, and did not begin to be restored until the 16th Century in the time of Martin Luther.

The emphasis of Luther's preaching was on God's provision, not on men's religious works. Since Luther's time, the many expressions of praise and worship mentioned in the Psalms have been practiced by the people of every major revival. Today, those who worship according to the pattern found in the Book of Psalms find that praise creates a canopy of the glory of God even as it did in David's day. Under this canopy of glory, the Church of our generation can expect the work of revival to spread from church to church and from nation to nation. The more we praise with sincere hearts the more the revival will grow. For where there is praise, God's power flows.

As God continues to restore the biblical pattern of praise and worship and more and more churches learn to worship in spirit and in truth, we will see the fulfilling of Jesus' prayer in John 17. Jesus prayed that the glory He had known with the Father before the world was created would be demonstrated to His disciples and then, through them, to all nations.

To me, the basic meaning of the word *glory* is that tangible evidence which supports the reputation that one has already heard of another. From the foundation of the world, God has had a reputation as an all-wise and mighty God, which is reinforced to us as believers when we see Him move sovereignly. Thus, Christ's prayer for His glory to be known is answered as the testimony of His works arises from all nations. And in the years of revival that are ahead of us, the day will come when the knowledge of the glory of the Lord will cover the earth as the waters cover the sea, Isaiah 11:9; Habakkuk 2:14.

Questions for this chapter on page 205

God's house of correction is His school of instruction.

Thomas Brooks, 17th Century English Puritan

We often learn more of God under the rod that strikes us, than under the staff that comforts us.

Stephen Charnock, 17th Century Puritan

A sanctified person, like a silver bell, the harder he is smitten, the better he sounds.

George Swinnock, English Puritan

Let us learn like Christians to kiss the rod, and love it.

John Bunyan, Puritan author/pastor

Affliction may be lasting, but it is not everlasting.

Thomas Watson, 17th Century Puritan

Chapter 7

AWAKENING THE CHURCH

As God continues His work of restoration, we will be brought to a place where God will awaken us to Bible truths that we have failed to see. The call to awaken has gone forth in our day, and the word of Ephesians 5:14, is being heard throughout the earth.

> *"Awake, thou that sleepest...and Christ shall give thee light."*

Again, the Church is showing signs of new life. Again, the heavenly vision which guided God's people in days of revival and restoration so often throughout history is shining brightly in the earth.

To be *asleep*, according to Ephesians 5, means to be blinded to truth and entangled in carnal things. The awakening of the Church can be likened to any normal morning when all creation begins to respond to the rising sun. Some are up long before the sun appears, and others awaken as the sun rises higher and the light shines more and more. Just as the natural creation awakens by degrees, here a little and there a little, so it is with the Church.

Awakening a sleeping Church does not come easily. As the voice of the Lord began to sound in my soul, "Awake, awake, and prepare for the hour is near for a new revival," I soon learned how painful it is for believers to wake up. The degree of pain in our awakening will be determined by the measures to which God must go in obtaining our complete attention. One method by which He awakens the Church and gains the attention of His people is through His judgments.

God's Judgments

When we find the word judgment in a passage of scripture, we must determine whether the reference is to eternal judgments or corrective judgments. *Eternal judgments* are the punishment for fallen angels, the devil, and all human beings who follow his wicked ways. God's *corrective judgments* are one of the means by which He teaches us to walk step by step, in His truth. The corrections, or chastenings, of the Lord are always meant to produce the peaceable fruit of righteousness in His people, Hebrews 12:5-11.

Much confusion exists among believers today because of the careless misuse of the word judgment. Many, not knowing what they are doing, have lumped all Bible statements referring to judgments under the eternal-punishment classification. This results in their losing sight of God's patient, loving, gentle, persistent dealings in correcting the ways of His people to make them useful instruments in His kingdom. When we are led to think that every line of scripture using the term judgment refers to our repeated appearance before the judge to once more be told, "You've failed, and this is your punishment," we are soon turned off and go to sleep spiritually — especially when we identify the minister as the judge and our every appearance in church as a time of reprimand and sentencing.

Eternal judgments

Only the wicked dead will appear before the throne for eternal judgment to be sentenced and banished from the presence of the Lord. All who are yet alive in the flesh are invited to come boldly to the throne of grace where Jesus ministers God's corrective judgments and continually fulfills the word of Matthew 12:20: He sends forth judgment unto victory. When God's corrective judgments are ministered to us by the loving hand of Jesus, there will be victory; then awakening out of sleep will no longer be painful. Awakening will be a joyful restoration and a revelation that we are part of a triumphant army.

Corrective judgments

Peter was referring to corrective judgments when he said that judgment must begin at the house of God, I Peter 4:17. According to Isaiah 51:4, God's corrective judgments are enlightenment and they are designed to bring us to a place where we will walk in His purposes.

The following scriptures help us to understand how the judgments of God work in our favor and aid in preparing the Body of Christ to go on to perfection and obtain peak level of revival.

> *"He is the Rock, his work is perfect: for all his ways are judgment: a God of truth and without iniquity, just and right is he."* Deuteronomy 32:4.

Corrective judgments are God's principles

To say that *all God's ways are judgment* signifies that His judgments are the principles He applies to correct us and cause us to walk in obedience to His Word.

Isaiah 4:4 says that the Lord will take away the uncleanness from His people by the spirit of judgment and the *spirit of burning*. The *spirit of judgment* refers to the work of the Holy Spirit as He applies God's ways and principles to men's hearts. The spirit of burning is the "burning anointing" that gives unction for teaching and preaching. Thus through anointed teachers God applies His corrective judgments with such force of the Spirit that our own thoughts and ways are purged out of our hearts and God's Word and His ways are engraved on our hearts and minds.

> *"A bruised reed shall he not break, and the smoking flax shall he not quench: he shall bring forth judgment unto truth,"* Isaiah 42:3.

God's corrective judgments apply His truth to our lives. Jesus, quoting Isaiah 42:3, gives us further understanding as He spoke of His own ministry and said that God sends forth judgment unto victory. Matthew 12:20. When God's truth triumphs over our ways, the corrective judgments of the Lord have made us to shine as lights among the nations.

> *For it is God which worketh in you both to will and to do of his good pleasure. Do all things without murmurings and disputings: That ye may be blameless and harmless, the sons of God, without rebuke, in the midst of a crooked and perverse nation, among whom ye shine as lights in the world,"* Philippians 2:13-15.

In Daniel 7:26 we find a good Bible example of how God's corrective judgments are sent forth unto victory. Daniel said that when the judgments are set, that is, when God's ways and principles are firmly set into our lives controlling our attitudes and conduct, then we, the people of God, will take away the dominion of the oppressor and we will possess the kingdom of God unto the uttermost parts of the earth.

We learn from Psalm 149 that all God's people have the honor to execute God's judgments upon the heathen. This means that as we walk in God's ways, our daily lives will so effect the people of the world around us that Satan's power will be bound and they will be free to come to Christ.

Corrective judgments prepare us for revival

The scripture in Revelation 10 is a perfect example of corrective judgments:

> *"And I saw another mighty angel* [messenger] *come down from heaven, clothed with a cloud: and a rainbow was upon his head, and his face was as it were the sun, and his feet as pillars of fire. And he had in his hand a little book open.... And cried with a loud voice, as when a lion roareth: and when he had cried, seven thunders uttered their voices,"* Revelation 10:1-3.

The word *thunder* in the Greek language means that a clear proclamation has been made. These proclamations are the voice of God calling for corrective measures to awaken the Church. They are seven in number because seven in Bible numerics is the number of a complete work, a work that brings us into God's rest where our faith is operating on a supernatural level.

Corrective judgments are like the alarm on a clock; they are used to awaken a sleeping Church. God only resorts to the use of corrective measures as an alarm when we will not awaken at the call of His voice. The Holy Spirit uses the circumstances of life and the teaching of Bible truths to help us press into greater victories. This is the same principle as the "times of shaking" referred to in Haggai 2:7 and Hebrews 12:26,27, where everything that is not anchored in truth is shaken, leaving only that which cannot be shaken.

Revelation 10:4 gives us further insight:

> *"And when the seven thunders had uttered their voices, I was about to write: and I heard a voice from heaven saying unto me, Seal up those things which the seven thunders uttered, and write them not."*

The apostle John was told not to write out the details of the seven proclamations. When God seals a word in the Scriptures, He reserves the right to reveal it later to whom He will and when He will for His own purposes. The same principle is taught in Isaiah 8:16,17:

> *"Bind up the testimony, seal the law among my disciples. And I will wait upon the Lord, that hideth his face from the house of Jacob, and I will look for him."*

Habakkuk 2:3 is similar:

> *"For the vision is yet for an appointed time, but at the end it shall speak, and not lie: though it tarry, wait for it; because it will surely come, it will not tarry."*

These seven corrective judgments of Revelation 10 are clearly in the classification of scriptures that God applies anytime the occasion calls for it.

Does God give us a clue as to the proper timing when he applies corrective judgments? Yes. We read in Revelation 10, verses 6 and 7:

"...that there should be time no longer: But in the days of the voice of the seventh angel, when he shall begin to sound, the mystery of God should be finished, as he hath declared to his servants the prophets."

The phrase, "there should be time no longer," is properly rendered from Greek, *"time shall be no longer delayed."* Thus, the idea conveyed in these verses is that time shall be no longer delayed for "the mystery of God" to be finished as God has declared to the prophets.

The Mystery of God

The phrase *the mystery of God* always refers to any portion of Scripture which is difficult to understand. When it is time for that truth to be applied in our lives, the Holy Spirit will then reveal it. A mystery is simply a secret truth — a truth that was in the Scriptures all the time. The specific mystery referred to in Revelation 10 is God's plan for completing restoration in the Church and sending revival throughout the earth. Although this plan was spoken of here a little and there a little by all the prophets, yet it remained a mystery to most believers in their generations until the time appointed by the Father to build up Zion. When it is time for revival there will be no more delay. God will reveal His plan to bring corrective judgments and restore the Church to truth — the kind of truth that brings sweeping revival. He first reveals His plan of restoration to the remnant of His people who are earnestly seeking to know God's purposes in their generation. Then they spread the word among all the people.

We can see how this has been happening over recent years. First small groups here and there began to understand that it was time for another revival in the Church. These small groups spread the word to others, and now nationally and internationally respected television ministries are being led of the Father to emphasize the fact that it is time for a new wave of revival.

God's timing

Many scriptures show that God has appropriate times when He deals in restoration. These times are not bound by the calendar year, but are reserved in the Father's own power to apply any time He chooses. Jesus made this clear in Acts 1:6,7:

> *"When they therefore were come together, they asked of him, saying, Lord, wilt thou at this time restore again the kingdom to Israel? And he said unto them, It is not for you to know the times or the seasons, which the Father hath put in his own power."*

Restoration is not a one-time event

Jesus made clear to the disciples that the restoration of the kingdom is not a one-time event set on a calendar in heaven, which will only take place after the appropriate years have come and gone. He showed them that the restoration of the kingdom takes place every time the Spirit of God is poured out and God's servants arise and preach the gospel of the kingdom. It was only ten days after the disciples had asked the question when the first New Testament restoration of the kingdom commenced. As the Spirit was poured out on the day of Pentecost, Peter stood up with the eleven and preached the gospel of the kingdom and immediately three thousand Jewish believers were restored to the kingdom through the new birth, Acts 2.

Since the day of Pentecost, the Holy Spirit has been poured out in times of refreshing again and again, generating one wave of revival after another, and each time restoring the kingdom life to believers among the nations.

The following scriptures show us that God's plan for world evangelism includes many times of restoration:

> *"Repent ye therefore, and be converted, that your sins may be blotted out, when the **times of refreshing shall come from the presence of the Lord;** and he shall send Jesus Christ, which before was preached unto you: Whom the heaven must receive until **the times of restitution** [restoration] **of all things, which God hath spoken by the mouth***

of all his holy prophets since the world began." Acts 3:19-21.

*"Thou shalt arise, and have mercy upon Zion: **for the time to favor her, yea, the set time, is come.** For thy servants take pleasure in her stones, and favor the dust thereof. So the heathen shall fear the name of the Lord, and all the kings of the earth thy glory. **When the Lord shall build up Zion, he shall appear in his glory.** He will regard the prayer of the destitute, and not despise their prayer."* Psalm 102:13-17.

*"And **I will restore to you the years** that the locust hath eaten, the cankerworm, and the caterpillar, and the palmerworm, my great army which I sent among you."* Joel 2:25.

*"But this is that which was spoken by the prophet Joel; And it shall come to pass **in the last days, saith God, I will pour out of my Spirit upon all flesh:** and your sons and your daughters shall prophesy, and your young men shall see visions, and your old men shall dream dreams: and on my servants and on my handmaidens **I will pour out in those days of my Spirit;** and they shall prophesy: **and I will show wonders in heaven above, and signs in the earth beneath;** blood, and fire, and vapor of smoke: the sun shall be turned into darkness, and the moon into blood, before that great and notable day of the Lord come: And it shall come to pass, that whosoever shall call on the name of the Lord shall be saved."* Acts 2:16-21.

*"**In that day will I raise up the tabernacle of David** that is fallen, and close up the breaches thereof; and I will raise up his ruins, and I will build it as in the days of old: That they may possess the remnant of Edom, and of all the heathen, which are called by my name, saith the Lord that doeth this. Behold, **the days come, saith the Lord, that the plowman shall overtake the reaper,** and the treader of grapes him that soweth seed; and the mountains shall drop*

*sweet wine, and all the hills shall melt. And **I will bring
again the captivity of my people** of Israel, and **they shall
build the waste cities,** and inhabit them; and they shall
plant vineyards, and drink the wine thereof; they shall also
make gardens, and eat the fruit of them. **And I will plant
them upon their land,** and they shall no more be pulled up
out of their land which I have given them, saith the Lord
thy God."* Amos 9:11-15.

According to the scriptures that bear on corrective judgments, a
time of worldwide shakings and divinely applied corrective measures
will be required to awaken a carnal, lukewarm, sleeping Church. As
God moves in preparation to bring forth the Church from its cocoon,
so that it may spread its wings of glory and reveal Christ's beauty to
the world, there will need to be times of distress and perplexity.

Avoid negative viewpoints

We must be careful that we do not fall into a negative human
viewpoint during times of distress, thinking that "Armageddon" is
just around the corner. Throughout history both those who expected
"Armageddon" any day and those who awakened to revival have
lived side by side. Sadly, it is observed that many have missed the
revival in their generation, being blinded by the fear of coming
holocaust because they thought corrective judgments were the beginning of eternal judgments.

An example of how such a time of distress preceding the birthing
of a fresh work of God is seen in the story of the prophet Jonah. Both
Jonah and the men on the ship with him had to go through a great
storm in order for God to set the stage for Jonah's ministry to be
effective. How effective was his ministry? Very effective, indeed.
More than two hundred thousand souls turned to the Lord.

Once we understand how revival begins during a time of distress,
we can then look at distress in any nation and see it as a sign that the
Holy Spirit will soon begin a new work in men's hearts. And out of
that remnant a revival harvest will ultimately come. Korea, Indonesia,
Nigeria, and even Red China are examples in recent years of this fact.

Understanding this is a key that opens the door to a positive, hope-filled future.

As we return to the scriptures in Revelation 10, we see how appropriate the words of verses 8 and 9 are to our time. Today as never before the voice of the Lord is being heard saying, *"...Go and take the little book....Take it, and eat it up...."* Eating the little book is symbolic language, which speaks of the willingness of heart to accept God's corrective measures with a positive response, knowing that in so doing we will receive restoration and revival in our own lives. Never has there been a more appropriate time to "eat" the little book and experience restoration. When we do and the corrective judgments of God have prepared the Church for a new revival, we will be able to go again and speak the word of the Lord to many nations, tongues and kings, as we are commanded to do in Revelation 10:10,11.

Why must there be delay?

In closing this chapter, let us answer the questions that must come to each of us sooner or later. Why must there be delays in God's plan to bring the nations to Himself? What prevents God, or His people, from fulfilling His plan right now? Why are there times of delay? What is God waiting for? Does he change His mind from time to time? Are there certain times preordained to send revivals and the rest of the time there is no hope?

I believe the answers to these questions can be found in the fact that we are laborers together with God. For God to work His works, He must have prepared servants through whom He can work. Further, since the plan of God is to reach all peoples of the earth, He needs more than one or two well-prepared servants. Revival will be delayed only as long as it takes to fully prepare enough laborers to bring in the harvest.

In most cases, it takes years of preparation to remove hindering factors from our lives and prepare us to march as God's restored army. During the delay period God is working to bring us into greater unity so that he might bring us as one mighty army into the harvest fields. No one ministry can reap the whole earth.

We can expect God to deal with us much as He dealt with David and his mighty men during their waiting period after David's first anointing before he finally came to the throne years later. During the intervening years, the alarm was heard in David's camp from time to time, awakening him and his men to more and more truth which was so necessary to bring the whole kingdom into one accord. David and his mighty men were then able to conquer all their enemies and bring peace in all their borders. Then during the reign of Solomon, the knowledge of the glory of the Lord filled the whole earth, I Kings 10:24.

Many are awakening even now as God prepares us for the greater works that are to come. The Lord will continue to carefully apply the sevenfold corrective judgments to the Church of this generation. He will bring us to a place where we will also be awakened to all truth necessary for revival to spread throughout the earth.

Questions for this chapter on page 207

Hope is never ill when faith is well.

John Bunyan

Where reason cannot wade there faith may swim.

Thomas Watson

Faith is seated in the understanding, as well as the will. It has an eye to see Christ, as well as a wing to flee to Christ.

Thomas Watson

Where sin abounded, grace abounded much more.

Romans 5:20

When He first the work begun,
Small and feeble was His day:
Now the word doth swiftly run,
Now it wins its widening way:
More and more it spreads and grows,
Ever mighty to prevail:
Sin's strongholds it now o'erthrows,
Shakes the trembling gates of hell.

Charles Wesley (1794 hymn)

Chapter 8

A GOOD REPORT

The good report has never changed: God has always had a good plan for man and an appointed time to build up His people and fulfill His plan.

"For the Lord is good; his mercy is everlasting; and his truth endureth to all generations." Psalm 100:5.

Always, in times of trouble, the Lord will revive His work and His right hand will save, Psalm 138:7. Always, when sin abounds, grace does much more abound, Romans 5:20. Always, when darkness is upon the earth and gross darkness upon the face of the people, the glory of the Lord will arise as light upon those of His people who have received the good report, Isaiah 60:2. Throughout the ages many giants of faith have arisen whose positive messages caused the good report to be heard throughout the earth.

Even though some men may expect only doom and gloom because of the troubled times they are experiencing, God will always be able to find men like Noah, Abraham, Moses, or the apostle Paul who will receive the good report. And these men, by that good report, will overcome in troubled times.

Jesus said that he would build His Church and the powers of darkness would not be able to prevail against it, thus illustrating His absolute confidence in the power of God's plan that good should overcome evil, Matthew 16:18. Again and again in His teachings, Christ applied the principles of good overcoming evil. He showed how every evil force that came against the timely fulfillment of God's plan in His life was met with God's mighty power. The good report never changes; God's power will never fail. Christ, the perfect man of faith, the force and life of every true revival, has given us a basis for a good report in every generation and the hope of recurring revival throughout the Church age. Since Jesus is the author and finisher of our faith, His viewpoint is always available and will always show us how good overcomes evil. A good report will overcome any evil circumstance surrounding our lives.

While Jesus did say that in this world we would have tribulation, he also hastened to add, *"...but be of good cheer; I have overcome the world,"* John 16:33. *Be of good cheer* is a divine mandate which in essence says that because we are victors in Christ, we shall triumph in all things.

> We can have good cheer even in the face of the rising floods of evil, for we know that greater floods of grace will always rise.
>
> Charles Finney
> 19th Century Revivalist

Good Overcomes Evil

Again and again, the picture of good overcoming evil is found in Luke 21, where Christ spoke of the events that would fulfill the age of law and usher in the new age of the Church. The disciples had asked when the temple would be destroyed, when the Jewish age would come to an end, and if there would be a sign so that they could know when the time drew near. Christ's answer went far beyond their questions. As is so frequently the case in the Scriptures, the manifold wisdom of God is often expressed in simple words having implications far beyond the letter of the text.

Not only is the wisdom of God evident in Christ's answers to the disciples, but the seven clear divisions He made in this teaching also reveal the principle of how the good report always overcomes evil. In each division of Luke 21, Christ spoke of troubled situations and negative forces that the disciples could expect to encounter; then He concluded each division with a good report. Thus in addition to giving us a teaching dealing with specific issues, Christ also gave us a true-to-life example showing that we should expect a good report and why we should believe that good will always overcome evil, Romans 12:21.

Birth pains

The principle of good overcoming evil can be seen in Matthew 24 and Mark 13, which are parallel accounts of Jesus' teaching in Luke 21. In these chapters the phrase, *"All these are the beginning of sorrows,"* follows Jesus' first description of events that would take place in the troubled times that were to come. When the phrase, *"...the beginning of sorrows,"* is researched in the Greek language, we truly get a good report, for *sorrows* means "birth pains." Thus Jesus taught that troubles and trials suffered in this world are to be understood as birth pains giving birth to greater manifestations of the kingdom of God in our lives.

Saints of all ages could testify of the fact that negative forces came against their lives from time to time. But they could also testify that through faith and patience they inherited the promises of God and discovered that the goodness of God was enough. They learned the principle that we, too, must learn if we are to experience revival now: At the exact point where good overcomes evil, revival is seen anew.

The scenario of good overcoming evil has been repeated again and again in generation after generation. Hebrews 11 chronicles the generations of men from Adam to Christ who all obtained a good report by faith. Revival is always the result of the work of the Holy Spirit through those who have obtained a good report and who know that neither present calamity nor threat of future calamity can cancel Christ's words:

> *"I am come that they might have life, and that they might have it more abundantly,"* John 10:10.

When will Christ come and give us a good report? When will He, the author and finisher of our faith, stand to our defense? David said that God will be our refuge and strength and a very present help in trouble, Psalm 46. Isaiah said that when the enemy rushes in like a flood, the Spirit of the Lord will raise up a standard against him. Isaiah 59:19. Jesus said:

> *"Lo, I am with you always, even unto the end of the world."* Matthew 28:20.

Luke 21

As we begin our study of the seven divisions of Luke 21 we will see that Jesus did not deny the presence of evil in this world, but neither did He build His doctrine and teaching on it. On the one hand some today say there is no good, and on the other hand some say there is no bad. In Luke 21 Jesus lists seven groupings of evil and negative things that are common among the nations. Then He preaches the gospel of good, and in most cases it only takes one line of the good report to nullify several lines of evil reports. Let us learn from Christ to clearly evaluate the evil in the world, yet not allowing it to dominate our thinking. Let us be good news messengers, lending our efforts to overcoming the evil of this world through the good report of God's kingdom working among the nations.

Signs from Heaven

We will first consider the good report found in Luke 21:8-11: "...and great signs shall there be from heaven."

> *"And he said, Take heed that ye be not deceived: for many shall come in my name, saying, I am Christ; and the time draweth near: go ye not therefore after them. But when ye shall hear of wars and commotions, be not terrified: for these things must first come to pass; but the end is not by and by. Then said he unto them, Nation shall rise against nation, and kingdom against kingdom: And great earthquakes shall be in diverse places, and famines, and*

*pestilences; and fearful sights **and great signs shall there be from heaven.***"

Please notice that in spite of the calamities mentioned in these verses, they conclude with the promise of hope: "...*and great signs* [supernatural tokens, wonders and miracles] *shall there be from heaven.*" Throughout Bible history, the great signs from heaven have been acts of sovereign intervention where God moved in special ways to preserve His people and further the purposes of His kingdom. When Moses led the children of Israel out of Egypt, there were many sovereign interventions.

Signs from heaven give us a good report so that we can have the confidence, courage and spiritual energy to rise up and possess the kingdom regardless of world conditions. These sovereign interventions, which Jesus said were to come in troubled times, include the many great revivals of history. We can also expect revival in the troubled times of our generation.

The Church had scarcely been established when we find, in the early Chapters of Acts, the apostles praying for signs and wonders so that they might have boldness to face persecution and continue to spread the revival to the ends of the earth. Saints of all ages should pray this same prayer during troubled times and should expect to see the same results.

> "*And now, Lord, behold their threatenings: and grant unto thy servants, that with all boldness they may speak thy word, by stretching forth thine hand to heal; and that signs and wonders may be done by the name of thy holy child Jesus. And when they had prayed, the place was shaken where they were assembled together; and they were all filled with the Holy Ghost, and they spake the word of God with boldness. And the multitude of them that believed were of one heart and of one soul...,*" Acts 4:29-32.

A testimony

The good report in Luke 21:12-15, is, "And it shall turn to you for a testimony...For I will give you a mouth and wisdom, which all your adversaries shall not be able to gainsay nor resist."

> *"But before all these, they shall lay their hands on you, and persecute you, delivering you up to the synagogues, and into prisons, being brought before kings and rulers for my name's sake. **And it shall turn to you for a testimony.** Settle it therefore in your hearts, not to meditate before what ye shall answer: **For I will give you a mouth and wisdom, which all your adversaries shall not be able to gainsay nor resist.**"*

Here we read that in spite of persecution, rejection, and being put on the spot by those who question us, we are not to be fearful or troubled, for this evil shall also be overcome by good. God promises to put words of such wisdom in our mouths that our adversaries will neither be able to argue with nor resist our testimony. Christ gives us a good report by the promise, *"And it shall turn to you for a testimony."* This simply means that we will have an opportunity to share the good news of God's work in the earth. All revivals are a result of God's people obtaining a testimony that God is at work in their lives.

Not a hair of your head shall perish

The good report continues in Luke 21:16-19, "But there shall not a hair of your head perish. In your patience possess ye your souls."

> *"And ye shall be betrayed both by parents, and brethren, and kinsfolk, and friends; and some of you shall they be caused to be put to death. And ye shall be hated of all men for my name's sake. **But there shall not a hair of your head perish. In your patience possess ye your souls.**"*

Although these verses tell of betrayal and hatred, yet we have Christ's promise that we will overcome evil with good, and not one hair of our heads will perish as we in patience possess our souls. Here we see an all-important ingredient to revival — patience. Patience working with faith gives the good report the needed time to bring an effective work among those who have had a negative response to their troubling circumstances. Since troubled times never last, patience will enable us to endure to the end of any time of trouble. Patience enables us to maintain a good report and respond readily and joyfully to a new day of revival.

Times of Gentiles fulfilled

The triumph of the good report continues in Luke 21:20-24 as Christ speaks of the times of the Gentiles being fulfilled.

> *"And when ye shall see Jerusalem compassed with armies, then know that the desolation thereof is nigh. Then let them which are in Judea flee to the mountains; and let them which are in the midst of it depart out; and let not them that are in the countries enter thereinto. For these be the days of vengeance, that all things which are written may be fulfilled. But woe unto them that are with child, and to them that give suck, in those days! for there shall be great distress in the land, and wrath upon this people. And they shall fall by the edge of the sword, and shall be led away captive into all nations: and Jerusalem shall be trodden down of the Gentiles, **until the times of the Gentiles be fulfilled."***

Perhaps this is the best of all the good reports in Luke 21, as Jesus tells us that violence against the nation Israel will come to an end. Throughout the Old Testament, God used Gentile nations to chasten Israel, but in Christ under the New Testament all people of Israel are set free and the punishment required by the law is fulfilled in Christ's sufferings. Luke 21 tells of the time of the fulness of the Gentiles, and Romans 9 and 11 tell of the time of the fulness of the nation Israel. The fulness of Israel and the nations comes as a simultaneous event at the end of the age.

Some people believe that the days of vengeance, spoken of in Luke 21:20-24, that were to come upon Jerusalem took place in 70 AD, and that the treading down has continued until now. Josephus, the historian, gave a graphic report of the total destruction of the city of Jerusalem in 70 AD. He told of the armies pulling back, after having surrounded the city for some time, and how, during the temporary pull back the Christians fled to the hills as Christ had told them to do. He also told how immediately thereafter, the city was destroyed and the temple was laid waste. Others believe the days of vengeance are to begin during the tribulation and continue to the end of the period of tribulation. In this teaching we are not concerning ourselves with one position or another, for people who hold either position can have revival right now. The important thing in this passage of scripture is that we have another example of God's power to make everything work together for our good.

The time of the Gentiles' fulness, Romans 11 says, is when the true olive branch (Israel) will be grafted back in. And Romans 9:28 tells us what will take place as Israel is grafted into Christ:

> *"...He will finish the work, and cut it short in righteousness."*

In Romans 11:12-15, we read that this good report will effect the whole earth in the same beautiful way that spring gives new life and new hope to all.

> *"Now if the fall of them be the riches of the world, and the diminishing of them the riches of the Gentiles; how much more their fulness? For I speak to you Gentiles, inasmuch as I am the apostle of the Gentiles, I magnify mine office: If by any means I may provoke to emulation them which are my flesh, and might save some of them. For if the casting away of them be the reconciling of the world, what shall the receiving of them be, but life from the dead?"*

Throughout the Old Testament, from the giving of the law to the prophecies of Malachi, the Lord told His people that if they did not walk in the faith of Abraham they would be broken off from the tree of faith and scattered to the ends of the earth. However, every time God warned of their scattering, He also promised their regathering.

The regathering of Israel is said by the prophets to be an ensign to the nations, Isaiah 11:10-12. Ensign does not mean a sign of the end of the world. The Hebrew word for *ensign* means "to give a signal." According to Romans 11, the return of the Jewish people to their homeland is a signal of world-changing events. Their return is a signal of life from the dead for all nations, as the nations that have been on the brink of worldwide holocaust are turned from their wicked ways to the Lord. This indicates that we will live to see the greatest revival thus far in history. Israel's return is also the preparation for their spiritual rebirth. Then Isaiah's prophecy will be fulfilled: A nation shall be born in a day, Isaiah 66:8. This spiritual rebirth will take place as Israel is grafted into Christ, the tree of faith, as a part of the eternal Church of Jesus Christ.

Let us not only see the return of the Jewish people to their homeland as a signal of Christ's second coming, but let us also see their return as a signal that the greatest outpouring of the Holy Spirit is now at hand.

Redemption draws near

In Luke 21:25-28, Jesus gives us another good report, "...look up, and lift up your heads; for your redemption draweth nigh."

> *"And there shall be signs in the sun, and in the moon, and in the stars; and upon the earth distress of nations, with perplexity; the sea and the waves roaring; Men's hearts failing them for fear, and for looking after those things which are coming on the earth: for the power of heaven shall be shaken. And then shall they see the Son of man coming in a cloud with power and great glory. And when these things begin to come to pass, **then look up, and lift up your heads; for your redemption draweth nigh."***

These verses speak of distress, perplexity, and men's hearts failing for fear. Again, the good report keeps us safe from fear and alarm in troubled times. Christ's command for us to lift up our heads is much like the command in Psalm 24:

> *"Lift up your heads...and the King of Glory shall come in."*

We learn from the Psalms that lifting up of the head means to open the doors and gates of praise. When our heads are lifted up in praise, we see the Lord of Hosts, the God of Battles, coming in power into the midst of His people to redeem and deliver us from every calamity. While doubtful men may cringe in fear seeing only those things that are coming to pass upon the earth, believers rejoice knowing that God's keeping power will never fail. Revival always comes when men lift their eyes to the Lord, for our help comes from the Lord who made heaven and earth.

The wonderful work of redemption is never more visible than during times of sweeping revival. Let us remember that Isaiah 60 tells us to lift up our heads and arise and shine during troubled times when darkness is on the earth; for then we will see great multitudes coming to Christ, Isaiah 60:3-5.

Kingdom of God is at hand

In Luke 21:29-33, Jesus gives us another good report: "The kingdom of God is at hand."

> *"And he spake to them in a parable; Behold the fig tree, and all the trees; When they now shoot forth, ye see and know of your own selves that summer is now nigh at hand. So likewise ye, when ye see these things come to pass, know ye that **the kingdom of God is nigh at hand.** Verily I say unto you, This generation shall not pass away, till all be fulfilled. Heaven and earth shall pass away: but my words shall not pass away."*

The kingdom of God is the rule and control of God in our hearts. Where God is in control, the fruit of the kingdom of God will be seen in righteousness, peace and joy in the Holy Ghost. Romans 14:17. As God's kingdom increases, revival occurs among the nations.

According to these verses in Luke, just as summer is near to spring, when the leaves first shoot forth, so the kingdom of God is near, and soon to be demonstrated, bearing the fruit of redemption in a mighty work of the Holy Spirit, when trouble is on every hand.

Jesus goes on to say that when we see calamities among the nations we are to know that, that generation will not pass away without seeing the word concerning God's kingdom fulfilled.

The good report in this passage of scripture is that the calamities among the nations will have the same effect on the kingdom of God as the warming temperatures of summer have on the growing fruit, causing the Word of God to become fruitful in the hearts of men. Knowing that the Word of God cannot pass away or return void, we know that a great harvest must come.

Watch and pray

Finally, Jesus exhorts us to watch and pray always.

"And take heed to yourselves, lest at any time your hearts be overcharged with surfeiting, and drunkenness, and cares of this life, and so that day come upon you unawares. For as a snare shall it come on all them that dwell on the face of the whole earth. **Watch ye therefore, and pray always, that ye may be accounted worthy to escape all these things that shall come to pass,** *and to stand before the Son of man."* Luke 21:34-36.

Jesus warns us in these verses to take heed to ourselves and to not allow the cares of life and the things that are coming upon the world to cause our hearts to become heavy or overly-concerned to the point that we lose our good report. It is truly the devil's trap to draw us into one evil report or another. Satan works constantly, using the cares of life as the basis of evil reports, causing many to believe that the Church is going down in defeat. Satan, who is the accuser and intimidator, makes it his business to keep believers so preoccupied with the cares of the world that we unknowingly lose our good report, sink into despair and lose the will to walk in victory. But God has clearly promised that we will be more than conquerors during these times. Therefore, the final good report is in the form of a promise that if we seek God's face we will be able to escape all the things that are coming on the earth. Revival is always possible when believers are earnestly praying and God is mightily working, keeping His people safe in troubled times. Our testimony is never more effective than when we have a good report during times of great distress. Our light is always the brightest when the world is the darkest.

Men of faith will always be able to find the good report. Though the good report be buried under mountains of rubble, faith will move those mountains.

Revival is always in the now for those who have obtained the good report. Let us be as the elders of Hebrews 11 and, by faith, lay hold upon the good report. Yes, the good report will be there; one needs only to search the Scriptures to see its light, to hear its song, and to be clothed in its strength and power.

Questions for this chapter on page 209

*False eschatologies, by surrendering history to the devil,
hastened the retreat of Christian influence and power.*

R.J. Rushdoony, author and historian

*Self-respecting scholars have committed one crucial error
which undermines their entire system of interpretation. Their
attention is focused on world conditions rather than on the
authoritative and unchanging promises of God. This
fallacy-ridden approach to prophecy has been rightly termed
"newspaper exegesis"—studying current events rather than
the Bible for clues to the future.*

David Chilton, *Paradise Restored*

*The sack of Rome by the Vandals (A.D. 410) was supposed to
bring on the end; the birth of the Inquisition (1209–1244)
prompted many well-meaning saints to conclude that it was the
beginning of the end; the Black Death that killed millions was
viewed as the prelude to the demise of the world (1347–1350).*

Gary DeMar, *Last Days Madness*

*What we are about to consider will tend to shew that, instead
of permitting ourselves to hope for a continued progress of
good, we must expect a progress of evil; and that the hope of
the earth being filled with the knowledge of the Lord before the
exercise of His judgment, and the consummation of this
judgment on the earth, is delusive.*

J.N. Darby, a lecture in 1840,
from *The Collected Writings of J.N. Darby*

Chapter 9

HINDRANCES TO REVIVAL

In this century, as throughout history, one of the major hindrances to revival has been the preoccupation of many believers with troubled world conditions and constant predictions of the end of the world. In many circles there has been so much excitement about the end of the world that it seems to have become the ultimate theme of the Bible in our generation. But the ultimate theme of the Bible has always been and will always be God's plan for the harvest of the multitudes in worldwide revival.

In the previous chapter we saw how Christ's positive vision for the last days always gives us a basis for hope despite negative world conditions. Christ did not teach us to deny existing troubled conditions. We are not to let our hearts be filled with care and sorrow because of world conditions, but we are to look up and lift up our heads for our redemption (His help) is near, Luke 21. God's plan of revival does not change when world conditions grow worse. In truth, the worse the conditions are in the world the brighter is the hope of revival. Each of us must decide whether we will adopt the viewpoint which says that present troubled world conditions signal the end of the world, or if we will learn from history that God has always intervened during times of great trouble in the world.

We of this century are still struggling with negative human reactions to troubled world conditions. And out of these reactions has come an overwhelming desire to predict the end of the world. Just as any form of impatience blinds believers to the orderly timings of God, so an impatient negative reaction to troubled world conditions blinds all who come under its sway. It is obvious that men everywhere, both those who are religious and those who are not, are blindly groping in attempts to predict the future and somehow find a straw of hope to cling to during these troubled days.

Believers whose thoughts are overly occupied with the troubled conditions among the nations have a tendency to rule out the positive hope of revival and actually go into a negative hope. They then become excited every time there is a new commotion among the nations, which they interpret as an evident sign that the end of the world is at hand. They have erred and turned God's ways upside down. For we are not to interpret the Bible according to world conditions; we are to interpret world conditions in the light of God's Word. II Peter 3:9 says that God is not willing that any should perish; He will finish His plan for world evangelism. A continual emphasis on the end of the world keeps our minds entangled with the negative conditions around us and makes it difficult for us to be channels of revival.

Our study of Luke 21 in Chapter 8, "A Good Report," clearly shows that the greatest sign of the second coming of Christ is a completely revived Church that has thoroughly fulfilled the great commission and exhaustively finished God's plan to bring the gospel to the nations of the earth. We need to let our hearts become settled in the knowledge that the Lord will come when the work is done and that no man can delay or hurry that day. He that shall come, will come, and will not tarry, Hebrews 10:37. And until He comes, God's covenant of grace and mercy through Jesus Christ stands sure.

To lose the hope of revival is to lose the exciting expectation that God is about to do something good. Truly, a life without the hope of revival is like receiving a life sentence with no hope of a reprieve. In truth, the rapture of the Church is not a last moment escape for imprisoned saints. Indeed, it is quite the opposite; it is the celebration day for a Church that has overcome all things.

The Second Coming of Christ

The Scripture is absolutely clear in its declaration that Jesus shall return to earth again. At His ascension the angels said:

> *"...This same Jesus which is taken up into heaven, shall so come in like manner...,"* Acts 1:11.

But Peter said that until the day dawns ... until the hour comes ...until the trump of God sounds, we are not to follow cunningly devised fables hoping that maybe tomorrow the Lord will come. Peter said that we should give heed to the more sure word of prophecy. That more sure word is Christ's own promise, "Lo, I am with you always," Matthew 28:20. When Jesus said, "I am with you always," He guaranteed that all believers in all generations could experience revival in their lifetimes.

The hope of Christ's return at God's appointed time in the future in no way conflicts with the hope of revival in the here and now. On the other hand, experiencing revival need not diminish the brightness of our hope that Christ will return at the end of the age. Equal emphasis should be placed on both the hope of revival and the hope of Christ's return, and revival should continue from generation to generation until the Lord does come.

Can we know when?

Can any man know the day and the hour of Christ's return? Is it possible for a Bible scholar to uncover secrets in the Scriptures that will give the exact day and hour of Christ's return? Could an angel from God give secret insight to us concerning the time of Christ's return? All of these questions are answered by the words of Jesus in Mark 13:32.

> *"But of that day and that hour knoweth no man, no, not the angels which are in heaven, neither the Son, but the Father."*

When Jesus, the Eternal Son of God, became the Son of Man, He emptied Himself of His eternal glory. This made possible a unique situation: Jesus Christ was both very God of very God and very man of very man. Though holding title to all eternal glory, Jesus was yet limited to that portion of the mind of the Father that was made available to Him during His earthly ministry — the mind of Christ.

The mind of Christ, according to New Testament theologians, is limited to the revealed Word of God canonized in the sixty-six books of the Holy Scriptures. All believers have been given the mind of Christ, I Corinthians 2:16. All that any man can ever know about God in this life is contained in the Word — the mind of Christ. How dare any believer think that he has more in his mind than that which is in the mind of Christ. How dare any man presume that he has found a secret in the Scriptures which reveals the day of Christ's return when Jesus said that He did not know, nor does any man know, the day of His return, Mark 13:32. If the Son of Man does not know the day and the hour of His return, then this information is excluded from the mind of Christ and is therefore excluded from the Bible, for surely Christ both knew and understood thoroughly every word of the Scriptures.

When we lose sight of the present hope of revival, we begin to think that the second coming of Christ is the only answer for our time. In our desperation to grasp any straw of hope, we are often found clinging to human theories instead of God's Word.

Is date-setting wrong?

Some have thought that since the Lord will ultimately come, there is no harm in trying to determine the time of His return. However, each time someone sets a date for the second coming of the Lord and it fails, as it must, there is a loss of hope and belief in the validity of the Bible. Many believers become disillusioned; some even leave the church completely. Others lose the strength of faith and stumble and falter for years in their disappointment that Christ did not return. Furthermore, multitudes in the world look upon Christians as foolish people who do not know what they are talking about.

Many who preach that the world will end soon say that this helps bring people to Christ. They validate this by quoting Jude 23 which speaks of some being saved through fear. However, a close examination of the lives of people who are saved through fear reveals that they seldom become fruitful in the kingdom of God. Because their minds are being so entangled with negative world conditions, they neither expect revival nor expect to overcome in their everyday walk with Christ. With no expectation of daily victory, those birthed by fear are the targets of Satan's continual attack rather than being a testimony of God's mighty power working in their generation.

Unscriptural Theories

It would be helpful to take a closer look at some of the unscriptural theories which Satan has used to confuse innocent believers, for Peter said that the ignorant and unlearned often distort scriptures that are hard to understand. On the surface these distorted teachings often appear believable because they include scripture quotations. Yet they are similar to the attacks Satan brought against Jesus in the wilderness, as he quoted scripture but applied it incorrectly. Had Jesus followed the misapplied scriptures as they were set before Him by Satan, the revival that swept through His generation would not have happened. It is imperative that the Church in our generation put all theories concerning the second coming of the Lord to the strongest biblical test, and then we must take our stand on the Word of God as Jesus did. We cannot allow the revival in our generation to be thwarted by theories based on negative reactions to world conditions. While well-intentioned and sincere men have given us countless theories concerning the Lord's second coming, we only need to look at a few of the theories being taught today to see how easy it is to misapply scriptures when it comes to dealing with the time for the second coming of the Lord.

The Three-day Theory

This theory is based on the fact that Jonah was in the belly of the great fish for three days and nights and Jesus was in the heart of the earth the same length of time. The theory then goes that Hosea 6:2 is the scripture that reveals the meaning of the three days. *"After two days will he revive us: in the third day he will raise us up, and we shall live in his sight."* Then II Peter 3:8, which says that a day with the Lord is as a thousand years, is used as the basis for interpreting that the three days represent three thousand years.

This would put Christ's return at the end of two thousand years, with the following one thousand years being the millennial reign of Christ. But since our calendar varies from the Jewish calendar, the date should be adjusted back into this century a few years. Accordingly, some who put forth this theory thought that the calendars were off as much as fifty years and were convinced that Christ would come by the early 1950s. Others, thinking the calendar to be off only three or four years, are still using this theory to predict that Christ will come in the 1990s.

Those who incorrectly apply the promise of Hosea 6:2, which speaks of being raised up in the third day, to the second coming of Christ, miss the promise of great revival indicated in Hosea 6:3.

> *"Then shall we know, if we follow on to know the Lord: his going forth is prepared as the morning; and he shall come unto us as the rain, as the latter and former rain unto the earth."*

The latter rain speaks to us of the rain that precedes every great revival. If the raising up to *live in His sight* in the third day refers to the rapture of the Church, then the promise of latter rain would have no meaning. After the rapture of the Church, there will be no need for either former rain or latter rain upon the earth. Let us claim the harvest rain, for surely it is revival time again.

The Seven-day Theory

This supposition is based on the fact that God worked six days and rested on the seventh. Therefore, again using the equation of *one day is as a thousand years,* this theory states that after God has worked six thousand years in the human race (four thousand in the Old Testament dispensation and two thousand in the New Testament dispensation), Jesus will come and the seventh one-thousand-year period would then be the millennial reign of Christ.

While this theory sounds believable, again let us remember that it must be false, because no man knows the time of Christ's return.

However, the fact that God worked six days and rested on the seventh is not without meaning to New Testament believers. Based on biblical numerics the six days of labor speaks of human effort through the energy of the flesh outside of faith, and the seventh day speaks of the faith-rest in Christ. The seventh day speaks of the faith-rest available to all generations throughout the entire Church age. The teachings in Hebrews 4 shows us that the resting place of the Lord is upon the mercy seat, where all believers come for grace and help in the time of need. It is by the preaching of justification by grace through faith that the door of salvation is opened to all nations. Anywhere and anytime this message is preached and believed, there will be revival.

Twelve-Hours-in-a-Day Theory

This is another mathematical equation presumed to be a secret code in the Scriptures. This idea based on John 9:4, *"I must work the works of him that sent me, while it is yet day: the night cometh, when no man can work,"* and on John 11:9, *"Are there not twelve hours in a day?"* Many will remember that this theory predicted the second coming of Christ in the 1960s.

According to Bullinger's book on Bible numerics, the number twelve speaks of the government of the kingdom of God. Jesus is simply saying that we can work the works of God so long as we abide under the authority of God's kingdom. Beyond that realm of divine government, there is darkness where no man can work the works of Jesus. The Scriptures clearly teach that we are children of the light for we have been translated out of the kingdom of darkness into the kingdom of light. In God's kingdom there is no night, for Jesus is our light. The apostle James declared that there is no darkness in Him at all.

The Generation Theory

> This idea suggests that the Lord will come in the same generation in which Israel again became a nation. According to the theory, Israel is the fig tree of Luke 21 and the return of the Jews to their homeland marks the beginning of the generation which would not pass away until Christ's second coming.

There are several discrepancies in this theory. To start with, some say Israel became a nation in 1912, some say 1918, and others 1948. Even more confusion exists in this theory because some say a generation is forty years, some thirty, others twenty. But the Scriptures do not give the length of a generation. The length of a generation varies according to the longevity of the majority of the people. Also, while most Bible scholars believe that the fig tree refers to the nation Israel, this is a "doctrine of deduction," for the Bible does not say this specifically.

A doctrine based on deduction cannot hold the same authority as an actual statement of Scripture. A deduction is a conclusion drawn by comparing one scripture with another. Doctrines of deduction are also formed by comparing one thought with another, and then selecting the more logical thought and concluding that it is the truth.

Since we know no scripture can give us the day and the hour of the Lord's return we must take a closer look at Luke 21:29. *"...Behold the fig tree, and all the trees."* This verse not only speaks of the fig tree but of all the trees of the field. Luke 21:30 goes on to say that when we see the fig tree and all the trees budding we can know that summer is near. (According to Jeremiah 8:20, summer is the time of harvest.) Then Luke 21:31 says that when we see these things come to pass we know the kingdom of God is at hand. The phrase *is at hand* in the original text, means "is happening right now." Jesus is literally saying that when we see all the signs of harvest time we will know that this generation will not pass away until all the harvest is brought in. Luke 21:32 does not say that this generation will not pass away until the Lord returns to the earth; it says *"until all be fulfilled."* Since we know that God works in times and seasons, and since this verse is speaking of harvest time, the "all things being fulfilled" most clearly speaks of a cycle being fulfilled in the harvest. The Word further says:

"...Thrust in thy sickle, and reap: for the time is come for thee to reap; for the harvest of the earth is ripe. And he that sat on the cloud thrust in his sickle on the earth; and the earth was reaped." Revelation 14:15,16.

All Scripture rises to teach us that every generation may reap the harvest of the earth in their lifetime. More emphasis is needed on harvest time and revival time than on the end of the world.

No man can hold back the day of Christ's coming. No man can hurry that day. Neither can any man predict that day. But all men must hear the message: Today is the acceptable day. The fields are white unto harvest, but the laborers are few. Reapers are needed for the signs of harvest are all around us.

Seventy-Weeks-of-Daniel Theory

This theory also is an effort of man to find some mathematical equation in Scripture which would predict the exact time of Christ's return.

The prophecy in Daniel 9 which speaks of the seventy weeks has many deep and wonderful meanings that edify believers. Yet we have no biblical authority to take this great prophecy and apply it to the second coming of Christ.

This prophecy in Daniel 9 was dealing with the first coming of Christ and gave an accurate timetable that began with the rebuilding of the temple in Ezra's day and was completely fulfilled in the death and resurrection of Christ. Since there are no scriptures to indicate that Daniel's timetable applies in any way to the second coming of Christ, we dare not force on these verses of scripture a theory that sounds good to our natural understanding. According to Mark 13:32, no man can know the day and hour of Christ's second return. Obviously then, no timetable in the Scripture can be legitimately used as a basis to establish the time of Christ's return.

Instead of looking to the Book of Daniel for a timetable which predicts the second coming of Christ, let us see the picture of God's eternal kingdom. In Daniel 7 we see that the kingdom of God would be set up on earth in Daniel's generation. This kingdom would have a dominion that would reach out to all peoples, nations and languages in such a way that ultimately all nations would serve the Lord. God's dominion is an everlasting dominion which shall not pass away and His kingdom is one which shall not be destroyed, Daniel 7:14.

These clear and reassuring scriptures give us great hope for revival. For even though nations collapse and human culture corrupts and decays, the kingdom of God continues from generation to generation. Jesus is King, we are members of the kingdom, and revival is the automatic result of God's will being done on earth in His kingdom as it is done in heaven. Let us not wait to go to heaven to find God's will. Revival is even now at the door.

Noah's Ark Theory

The basis for this popular theory is that when Noah's ark is found and measured, we will have an accurate measurement for a Bible cubit. With this information, so the theory goes, we could then use the measurements of the ark to work out a timetable to determine the second coming of Christ.

Even though Noah's ark may someday be reached and measured by the many teams of archaeologists who search on Mount Ararat for its resting place, the theory still lacks a biblical basis and cannot establish the time of Christ's return. The discovery of Noah's ark will be a blessing to all who believe the Bible and will settle the doubts of many who question the story of Noah and the ark. We look forward to that day with anticipation.

Alignment-of-the-Planets Theory

This theory states that twice in history certain planets were aligned for a period of time, supposedly at Noah's flood and again at Christ's birth. Thus, according to the theory, the third alignment of these planets would signal the second coming of Christ.

This theory was first brought to my attention in the early 1950s and then reappeared in the mid-1960s. Another appearance of this theory in the late 1970s was even more widespread. At that time the theory was given a certain respectability with the publishing of a book called *The Jupiter Effect*.

The authors of *The Jupiter Effect* said that a rare alignment, or grouping, of planets would take place in 1982. They claimed that this grouping of planets would cause a tidal influence on the sun, thus provoking a time of maximum sunspot activity which would trigger violent earthquakes.

The authors of *The Jupiter Effect* did not link their theory with the end of the world or the second coming of Christ. Sincere, but uninformed, Christians took the basic theory of the book and linked it to such catastrophic events as the submergence of California into the Pacific Ocean, as well as Christ's second coming and the end of the world.

Obviously, the theory of the alignment of the planets and its role in the second coming of Christ has been proven false. The year 1982 has come and gone, and the Lord has not returned. In addition, one of the authors of *The Jupiter Effect*, John Gribbin, publicly stated that the theory in their book had been proven wrong. See *Omni Magazine,* June 1980. Yet the theory persists in many circles.

Christians are warned throughout the Bible not to base religious teachings on stars and planets. These heavenly bodies, according to Scripture, are to give man natural light not spiritual light. When Christians transgress the clear commandment of the Bible and teach that in some way our lives as believers are influenced by the sun, moon or stars, we have left the clear teaching of Scripture and entered into the realm of cunningly devised fables of the occult.

When we as believers are caught up with predictions of doom and disaster, it is all too easy for us to think that our only hope is the second coming of Christ. We can become so caught up in praying for Christ to come soon that we fail to go into the world and preach the gospel as Christ has commanded.

The collapse of men's theories

The collapse of men's theories is always a signal that brings joy to the hearts of those who know their Bibles. They know that when men's wisdom fails, God's wisdom will shine forth like a light in the night and will restore order to the hearts of true believers, I Corinthians 1:21-31.

The collapse of anything in this world's system always signals the time for the Lord to work in His mercy in special ways. That is why Jesus told us to look up when we see things around us shaking, Luke 21:28. What if our money system were to crash? Would that be a sign of the end of all things? No. It would simply be an opportunity for God's people to arise and shine.

When earthly things are shaking and men's theories are collapsing, we are assured of a dwelling place under the shadow of the Most High. This is the place of full joy where we know that our enemies will be turned back and will fall at God's presence. While mountains are melting, systems of the world are being uprooted, enemies of God are fleeing, and nations are trembling, the just Lord will still be in the midst of His people. He will do no iniquity. He will not fail, Zephaniah 3:5. His people will arise and shine, and we will march like a mighty army treading down every hindrance in our path.

All hindrances to revival can be removed in this generation if we will act in the faith of Elisha who healed the pot of poison as he sprinkled it with the meal, which symbolizes the application of the Word of God to evil circumstances of world conditions, II Kings 4:38-41. If we will study the Word and apply it in faith, all poisonous pots filled with the unsavory viewpoints of human theory will be healed and multitudes who are trapped in a negative viewpoint will be set free. Christ's prayer "Thy kingdom come, thy will be done," will only be answered as we come into balance in every area of our lives. Overemphasis in any area is a hindrance to revival. Revival is the effective work of God's Spirit conforming both individuals and the masses to the will of God on earth as it was preordained in heaven before the world began.

During my lifetime we have come through several periods of negative predictions made by those in the Church and in the world. Again and again I have witnessed the failure of negative predictions declaring that the worst is yet to come and the end of the world is at hand. And following the collapse of these predictions, I have witnessed the appearance of revivals in various parts of the earth. Undoubtedly, negative predictions will appear again and again. But each time they do, we can make the decision to follow the words of Philippians 4:8,9.

"Finally, brethren, whatsoever things are true, whatsoever things are honest, whatsoever things are just, whatsoever things are pure, whatsoever things are lovely, whatsoever things are of good report; if there be any virtue, and if there be any praise, think on these things...and the God of peace shall be with you."

Let us join the ever increasing numbers of believers who are turning from a fearful and negative reaction to world conditions and turning to a joyful anticipation of the greatest revival in history.

Questions for this chapter on page 211

Some of the best impulses for social reform in America's history have come from awakenings. The anti-slavery movement in America was mainly a part of the reform movement generated by the Second Great Awakening, as were movements for prison reform, child labor laws, women's rights, inner-city missions, and many more.

Christian History, Vol. VIII, Spiritual Awakenings in North America

During the Third Great Awakening of 1857 to 1859, 10,000 people in New York City alone gathered together daily—even left work—to pray. The same thing was taking place all over the country, in small towns as well as in great cities.

Christian History, The Time for Prayer

The influence of the awakening was felt everywhere in the nation. It first captured great cities, but it also spread through every town and village and country hamlet. It swamped schools and colleges. It affected all classes without respect to condition. . . . It seemed to many that the fruits of Pentecost had been repeated a thousandfold. . . . the number of conversions reported soon reached the total of fifty thousand weekly. . . .

J. Edwin Orr, historian, concerning the Awakening of 1858

Chapter 10

RESTORATION REVIVALS

Years ago when I first heard the term, "restoration revival," I did not understand it. "Who needs a restoration revival?" I said, "just give us a revival!" Since then I have come to understand that there are different kinds of revivals. There are revivals in the breach, which are spasmodic on-and-off revivals; then there are revivals that repair the breach and restore Bible order — restoration revivals.

Repairing the Breaches

Repairing a breach is like rebuilding the walls of a city. Ezra and Nehemiah repaired the walls of the city of God in their generation and saw the glory of God restored. Theirs was not an easy task, but they had a burning desire in their hearts to see the city of God restored so that it would once again be a testimony among the nations. They remained faithful to the vision God had given them, and the revival in their day stands out as one of the greatest in Scripture.

While Ezra and Nehemiah repaired both spiritual and natural breaches in their day, we are dealing primarily with the spiritual realm. Breach is defined in *Webster's Dictionary* as "a failure to observe the terms; an opening made by breaking something; a gap; an interruption in friendly relations." In Nehemiah 4:7, the breach spoken of was a broken down area in the wall of Jerusalem. Numbers 14:34 speaks of a breach of promise, and this refers to a break in relationship between man and God. This kind of breach in the spirit exists where Bible order is not practiced, Proverbs 15:4.

On-and-off revivals

A breach occurs in the spirit when men fail to follow God's ways. Revivals that only stir the heart with joy but do not restore the heart to obey God and walk in His ways will never last. When the breach is repaired and we learn to walk in God's ways, we will come out of the on-and-off revival syndrome and into a state of continuous revival. Thus, the compelling need facing the Church of this generation is restoration that will heal the breach.

The on-and-off revival syndrome is why churches sometimes revive for a time when a new pastor arrives. But sooner or later the revival burns out, and the people wonder what happened to their pastor. The problem is not the pastor. The problem is that the breaches were not repaired and Bible order was not restored.

From the fall of Adam, God has been at work to help man repair the breaches and restore complete fellowship in the Spirit. All good things in life come down to us from the Father above. They are ministered to us by the Spirit of God and received into our lives through the work of faith in a restored heart and mind.

God's order

In the beginning, God created Adam and Eve to enjoy His continuous presence in all of its glory. But even in that first paradise there was a certain order. The order was simple and easy to follow. God said, "You may partake of all but one tree in the garden." When Adam and Eve failed to follow that order, a breach occurred. Thus, they were the first to fall short of, or break away from, the glory of God.

God, however, did not forsake His creation. He came to them in their fallen state, shed the blood of an animal, and used its skin to make them a covering. But it was not the same as in the garden of Eden where they had enjoyed the continuous, tangible reality of God's presence.

Throughout the Old Testament era, God's presence was only manifested among His people for short periods of time and in appointed places, generally after an altar had been prepared and a sacrifice offered. Many great men of God, such as Moses, Elijah, Elisha and Samuel, were instruments to bring spiritual awakenings to the people, but they were not able to repair the breach in the spirit between God and man. Therefore the glory of God was seen only now and then.

During the reign of King David, many spiritual breaches were repaired and the glory of God shone forth in the midst of the people more often and for longer periods of time than at any other time in Israel's history. (See Chapter 6, "God's Glory in the Church Again.")

From the time of David on, any generation who followed David's order of worship enjoyed a continual manifestation of God's glory and power. But during times when David's order was forsaken, either partially or totally, the glory of the Lord was lost because of the breaches in the order of worship.

God's promise to David included the coming of Christ, who would be the seed of David to sit upon the throne of David to establish and order it forever. The generations from David until the coming of Christ looked forward to the One who would repair all breaches between God and man and bring in an era of grace in which man would not lose God's glory for every little transgression.

Many revivals throughout history

Throughout the Church age, the Church has experienced many revivals in which the glory of God has swept through communities and nations in tremendous spiritual awakenings. These revivals reemphasized and restored Bible truths to their generations. In the 16th Century, during the time of the Reformation, justification by faith was the great Bible truth being restored. In the 18th Century, the Wesley brothers and other ministers brought a restored emphasis on the Bible doctrines of grace and holiness. At the turn of the 20th Century, another reformation took place, emphasizing the work of the Holy Spirit and world evangelism. In the 1940s and 1950s, the Church experienced revivals emphasizing God's healing power. And more recently, the renewals of the 1960s and 1970s brought a restored emphasis on praise and the gifts of the Holy Spirit.

None of these revivals, however, did a complete work of restoration. And until all the breaches are repaired, there cannot be a continuous worldwide revival. Thus, new waves of revival and restoration are still needed in the Church today as many areas of spiritual truth yet remain to be restored.

Consider again the rebuilding of the walls of Jerusalem and the temple after the captivity in Babylon. Several waves of restorers had come to Jerusalem and worked. Yet when Ezra arrived, he still found many breaches in the wall and much unfinished work in the temple. The story of Ezra and Nehemiah so fits the situation in our day. Signs are everywhere that God is so moving again.

Waste Places

God has been raising up and preparing ministries that will repair the breach in this generation, just as He promised in Isaiah 58:12:

> *"And they that shall be of thee shall build the old waste places: thou shalt raise up the foundations of many genera-tions; and thou shalt be called, The repairer of the breach, The restorer of paths to dwell in."*

Repairers of the breach build up the old waste places. A waste place is like a field that was once fruitful, prosperous and produced nourishment for the people. But lack of rain causes fruitful fields to turn into dry and thirsty lands — waste places.

Waste places are also like buildings that have fallen into disrepair. If a wooden building is not renewed with a fresh coat of paint every few years, the exposed boards will begin to rot, and finally the building will fall apart and no longer be of benefit to man.

Many churches that were once centers of revival in past genera-tions have become waste places because the people have forsaken

God's order. But in this new day of restoration, many such waste places are being rebuilt.

We also read in Isaiah 58:12 that repairers of the breach raise up the foundations of many generations. These foundations are Bible truths taught in the past which were covered by the rubble of human reasoning and religious tradition. In today's new wave of restoration we are again clearing away the rubble which had buried the great Bible truths that men such as Martin Luther, John Wesley and Charles Finney preached with such clarity in their generations.

During each new wave of revival, God not only restores truth to the Church, but He puts the emphasis on truths that have been overlooked. As Jesus said, every teacher who is well taught in the kingdom will bring forth out of his treasuries both old and new things.

All Bible truth

In the past the Church has enthusiastically embraced each truth that God was bringing forth during times of revival. Often though, they became so engrossed with those truths that they built denominations around them. As a result we have many groups and denominations, each emphasizing some aspects of Bible truth and divine order to the exclusion of other equally important Bible truths.

Anytime a believer, a congregation or a denomination "camps" upon certain areas of Bible truth and refuses to move on into other areas of Bible truth, breaches occur, God's will is not completed, and the possibility of revival is limited.

The significance of repairing the breach, building up old waste places, and raising up the foundations of many generations is even more clearly understood in the light of New Testament scriptures dealing with restoration, such as Acts 3:19-21.

> *"Repent ye therefore, and be converted, that your sins may be blotted out, when the times of refreshing shall come from the presence of the Lord; And he shall send Jesus Christ, which before was preached unto you: Whom the heaven must receive* [retain] *until the times of restitution* [restoration] *of all things, which God hath spoken by the mouth of all his holy prophets since the world began."*

As breaches are repaired, a greater emphasis is placed on scriptures dealing with times of refreshing and restoration.

Our expectation of God's promise to restore does include hope for both our natural and our spiritual affairs. Today, true worshipers must worship God in Spirit and in truth, therefore a greater emphasis must be on the spiritual application of restoration. We will gain a clearer understanding of the kinds of spiritual breaches that must be repaired from the following Bible examples.

Breach of promise

A breach of promise is spoken of in Numbers 14:34:

> *"After the number of days in which ye searched the land, even forty days, each day for a year, shall ye bear your iniquities, even forty years, and ye shall know my breach of promise."*

The word *breach,* as it is used in this verse, carries the idea of a break in relationships and of disallowing, or making of no effect.

God had given a promise to the children of Israel that they could go in and possess the land. But at His appointed time for them to enter into their inheritance, they refused to go in. Their rebellious, "We-can't-do-it-now" attitude neutralized, or made of no effect for them, God's promise that they would go in and possess the land.

Likewise, God's Word says, *"...with his stripes we are healed,"* Isaiah 53:5; I Peter 2:24. However, if a man says, "I cannot be healed now," the promise of healing is made of no effect to *that* man in *that* situation and at *that* time.

Revival is indeed a massive work of healing, but it is healing of more than a physical body. Revival is a healing of the spirit, mind, soul and body and includes the healing of society at large. If we say that we cannot have revival now, we create a breach in the spirit; wherefore, we must repent and take a stand in faith. To stand in faith is to declare that we can have revival now and determine to do our part to walk in God's order as established by the Scriptures.

As we claim revival for our generation, let us claim all that God has promised His people. Let us be willing for the Spirit of God to lead us into all truth and to rebuild divine order in all things.

If we say, "But I want things to continue as before," and we refuse to change and move on with God, a breach will occur, and the manifestation of God's power will be decreased. We may continue to practice that which worked in the past, but we will no longer get the same results. At this point we may simply conclude that the revival is over.

But the revival could have continued had we been willing to move to a new administration in the Spirit and rebuild divine order in other areas. Restoration incorporates all Bible teachings. Continuous revival is possible when we move from one administration of the Spirit to another, as God wills.

Many years ago the Lord taught our congregation the need to rebuild divine order in all things as He led us through many differing administrations of the Spirit. See I Corinthians 12:4-6. Anytime we refused to leave a doctrinal position or an administration of the Spirit in which we were comfortable and move on to a new thing with God, a breach occurred and the revival flow was quenched.

Personal example

When God began to show me on a personal level the importance of moving from one administration of the Spirit to another, He did so in the realm of divine healing. He showed me that I was no longer gong to be healed through the laying on of hands. Instead, I was going to learn that there are other ways to receive God's divine restoration of the body. He showed me that I was going to be healed little by little as I came before the Lord daily in prayer and claimed my healing day by day.

But I protested, "I don't like that. Kathryn Kuhlman says that God always does a complete work. I like her way. I don't think this little-by-little is even biblical."

Then the Lord caused me to see that my personal healing was to be part of my promised land. He would lead me into my promised land of healing, as the children of Israel were led into their promised land, little by little, Deuteronomy 7:22.

I learned during that time that God also heals as we daily feed on His Word. We read in Proverbs 4:20-22 that God's Word is health to all our flesh. The Word of God has to be taken in and digested, and that takes time. It may take a long time for us to digest enough of the Word to heal some conditions.

One healing I received took five years. Another, fourteen.

Do It God's Way

An important lesson concerning another kind of breach is to be learned from David's unsuccessful first attempt to bring the ark of God into Jerusalem. II Samuel 6. David and his men were sincere. They were trying to do God's will. We could even say that they were desiring restoration. However, they were not moving in divine order. Instead of carrying the ark in the specific way God had instructed that it be carried, which was on the shoulders of the Levites, they placed the ark of God upon a cart pulled by oxen.

As David and his men journeyed towards Jerusalem with the ark upon the cart, one of the oxen stumbled and Uzzah reached out to steady the ark so that it would not fall. When he touched the ark, he fell dead.

"And David was displeased, because the Lord had made a breach upon Uzzah...," II Samuel 6:8.

Only trying to help

It almost seems unfair that God would strike down a man who was only trying to help. But God does not need help; He just needs people who will obey and follow divine order. God used such drastic measures with Uzzah because he was not of the priesthood and was forbidden to touch the ark. Uzzah ignored God's due order and did things his own way.

After Uzzah's death, David was afraid to continue his ascent to Jerusalem with the ark of the covenant. Instead, the ark was carried into the house of Obededom, where it remained for three months. During that time the Lord blessed the house of Obededom and all that he had.

Later, David learned why the first attempt to bring the ark to Jerusalem had failed. He discovered that in their zeal to get things going they had failed to consider that there was a right way to do them. This right way is called due order in Scripture:

> *"For because ye did it not at the first, the Lord our God made a breach upon us, for that we sought him not after the due order,"* I Chronicles 15:13.

As in David's day, it will take more than an increase in numbers and a building program to build revival. Restoration is the work of God that repairs the breaches in our lives. Those whom God uses to repair breaches are training and preparing people to take their rightful places in the priesthood, so that they can carry the ark of the Lord in due order. That is what happened in David's day, and it can happen in our day. God is raising up many repairers of the breach through whom He is teaching His people due order.

Ministries in the Breach

Two kinds of ministries are found in the breach. The first could be called a man-in-the-gap ministry. We read in Ezekiel 22:30 that God looked for a man to make up the hedge and stand in the gap. Moses is an example of a man who stood in the gap.

> *"Therefore he said that he would destroy them, had not Moses his chosen stood before him in the breach, to turn away his wrath, lest he should destroy them,"* Psalm 106:23.

Man-in-the-gap revivals

Man-in-the-gap revivals have certain characteristics that set them apart from the usual ministries. Miracles happen and many souls are saved through these kinds of revivals; however, they do not heal the breach. These revivals last only as long as the man lasts and go only where the man goes.

Billy Graham

Billy Graham is a modern-day example of a man-in-the-gap ministry. His meetings draw crowds of tens of thousands, with hundreds and sometimes thousands coming to the Lord in each crusade. This rule prevails wherever he goes in America or overseas.

Kathryn Kuhlman

Kathryn Kuhlman was a woman in the gap. The rule of her ministry was seen in the thousands who always attended her meetings and the dramatic healings and miracles that took place.

I do not say that such great men and women of God are in any way lacking or that their ministries are not in God's will. They are beacon lights pointing the way to still greater things in God's kingdom. Such ministries have brought us to where we are today, but they alone cannot bring worldwide revival. It will take the whole church standing in the gap and repairing the breaches before we can have worldwide, continuous revival.

Jesus

Sometimes Jesus is the only one who stands in the gap.

> *"And he saw that there was no man, and wondered that there was no intercessor: therefore his arm brought salvation unto him; and his righteousness, it sustained him,"* Isaiah 59:16.

Occasionally, the power of God is manifested powerfully in a church where routine and tradition have been the rule, and the only explanation is God's sovereign intervention. People begin to fall under the power of God, dramatic healings take place, and many people are saved. No one can explain what has happened except to say that the Lord simply took over and did it. But Jesus' appearances where He stands alone in the gap are all too brief. If revival is to continue in such times, more and more believers must arise and stand with him in faith.

I remember years ago that when God took over in that way in our services it was the greatest day of the year. For weeks afterwards, we smiled; for months afterwards we talked about how wonderful it had been. One day, though, I asked a question: Why does the Lord have to take over in our service in order for His power to be manifested? I thought that He was supposed to work with us as we worked with Him? Then I discovered that He has to take over sometimes because we do not walk in due order; therefore, we find it impossible to know the leading of the Spirit and are left with only our own programs.

The watchmen

God is moving the Body of Christ into a position beyond the on-and-off revivals in the breach. He is bringing us into an era of repairing the breaches and restoring the old waste places. This is a time when the watchmen stand side by side upon the repaired wall and where they see eye to eye. See Isaiah 52. Although on-and-off revivals may continue in some local settings, the overall emphasis in the Body of Christ is moving towards restoration and unity. Leaders in the Church are being united in the Spirit as never before. As we move deeper into this era of repairing of the breaches, more and more watchmen will take their places standing side by side with their brethren in Christ. Having caught the vision of unity and a worldwide harvest, these watchmen will say to one another, "Let us go forth and reap the harvest of the earth."

Balaam-type ministries

Another ministry that flourishes in the breach is that of Balaam. See Numbers 22-24. On the one hand, Balaam could touch God through offering sacrifices and receive the revelation of the Lord and minister the blessings of God's covenants. On the other hand, for the reward of error (for money), Balaam, when he so chose, would work with enchantments, speaking curses and bringing bondages.

Some Balaam-type ministries are like tyrants, holding people in fear that the blessings will stop flowing to them if they do not comply with every personal demand of the prophet. Other Balaam-type ministries, however, are not the threatening kind. Their angle is to put a price tag on the healings and miracles they minister. There is yet another style of Balaam ministry, that while claiming to be the voice of God and the true revealer of God's will, denies the blessing for the people by saying that the days of miracles are over.

Balaam ministries will continue only so long as there are breaches. But when all the breaches are repaired, there will be no place for the Balaams. There will be no place for a mixed spirit where the one ministering is sometimes biblical and other times unbiblical.

There will be no place for those who say, "It feels right and gets results, so who cares if it is Bible order or not?"

Any way to get the job done

The any-way-to-get-the-job-done idea is not good enough — and it certainly will not bring revival! Any work that is not accomplished through Bible order will not last. If we are to experience the repairing of the breach, and if we are to go on to the perfection of which Paul spoke, we need more than Balaam ministries to come in and tell us what we want to hear. Flattering words and pats on the back may keep us going for a time, but eventually the breaches will appear.

There will be no breaches and no Balaam ministries when due order is restored. Only in the breaches are the unclean able to pass in and out among us. Balaam ministries come out of a negative attitude of the self-life. We need to be on guard against a life ruled by negative attitudes. While Balaam ministries may only involve a small segment of the Body of Christ the Balaam attitude can easily overcome anyone.

For example, Bible order teaches us to return good for evil. But if we retaliate instead of turning the other cheek when someone maligns us or turns against us, then we are yielding to the Balaam-type nature of the flesh and we are seeking the reward of unrighteousness as did Balaam. Or if the person who maligned us gets into some kind of trouble later and we are glad and say, "He deserved it!" we are clearly yielding to the Balaam attitude of the carnal man.

Pastors, as well as individuals in a congregation, are susceptible to developing bad attitudes when people get upset and leave their church. If we find it difficult to wish such people well, and find it easier to say, "Why couldn't they have acted right and used their faith over here where we could have benefited from it?" we are being tempted with a Balaam attitude.

Humility and grace

Humility and grace are required to keep us from walking in the breach with a Balaam attitude. We need a constant firebath from the throne to keep us pure in love and charity so that we may, by God's grace, return good for evil.

As Balaam finally died by the sword at the hands of the people of God, so will Balaam attitudes and ministries die as the sword of the Word works in our lives to restore Bible order.

Breaches are being repaired. Waste places are being restored. Foundation Bible truths of past generations are being raised up again. And as they are, Balaam-type attitudes are dying throughout the kingdom of God. The repairing of breaches is bringing a new level of unity throughout the Body of Christ. Not only are Balaam ministries and attitudes removed when the breaches are restored, but the impact of revival is raised sharply as the unity of believers is brought about. Much is said about unity in our time, but unity will only come to pass as the breaches are repaired.

Seeing that God's plan includes repairing of breaches, we can expect the Holy Spirit to continue emphasizing this needy area of renewal. As we continue to intercede and wait before the throne of God, the Spirit of God will teach us what we must do in our generation. Our Lord will never fail, nor will He be weary of the work until all the breaches have been restored. The best days for the Church are yet to come.

Questions for this chapter on page 213

The angel fetched Peter out of prison,
but it was prayer that fetched the angel.

Thomas Watson

Prayer is nothing but the promise reversed, or God's Word
formed into an argument, and retorted by faith upon God again.

William Gurnall, 17th Century Puritan

A saint is to put forth his faith in prayer,
and afterwards follow his prayer with faith.

Vavasor Powell, 17th Century Puritan

If our prayers in church were actually spoken as though we
were talking to Christ face to face, sooner or later a spiritual
reality would begin to make itself known. . . And before we
know it, we see early signs of awakening. Revival and prayer
always go together. They are inseparably linked.

David R. Mains, *"Praying Boldly,"* taken from *Christian History*

Chapter 11

INTERCESSORY PRAYER

At times it may seem to God's people that they are cast aside, scattered among the heathen and without hope. Israel mourned when they were in Babylon because they thought there was no hope. Thinking that God had cast them off, they felt they could not sing the songs of Zion, (Psalm 137). Had they known the power of intercessory prayer, they would have joyfully sung unto the Lord, knowing that God was with them in Babylon as much as He was in Jerusalem. God has promised to hear our prayers and revive us in bondage (Ezra 9:8), revive us in the midst of trouble (Psalm 138:7), and revive us in times of wrath (Habakkuk 3:2).

An overview of world conditions today reveals that the whole world lies in wickedness, just as I John 5:19 says. This world condition is also described in Isaiah 60:2, which says that darkness will cover the earth and gross darkness the people.

However, lest we should look at the darkness in the world and think there is no hope for the nations throughout the earth, God was careful to place the solution for overcoming their darkness in the same verse:

> *"...but the Lord shall arise upon thee, and his glory shall be seen upon thee."*

Then in verses 3 through 5, God speaks of the Gentiles' coming to the light and of multitudes in the earth being converted. God's saving light coming upon a people is a direct result of the covenant of II Chronicles 7:14:

> *"If my people, which are called by my name, shall humble themselves, and pray, and seek my face, and turn from their wicked ways; then will I hear from heaven, and will forgive their sin, and will heal their land."*

This shows how intercessory prayer brings light to the nations. God is again calling intercessors throughout the earth to prepare for a worldwide spiritual awakening — an awakening that will result in the healing of many nations and the salvation of millions of souls.

> *"...the abundance of the sea shall be converted unto thee...,"* Isaiah 60:5.

The Healing of Nations

The healing of nations comes as answered prayer. The process which causes healing is revival. God forbid that we, the Church today, should sin against the nations of our day by failing to grasp this mighty principle.

Throughout the ages, intercessors have taken their place in the all-important chain of defenders as they have stood between the powers of darkness and the needy people of the earth. While it is true that the devil has come down to the earth with great wrath and has declared his intentions to destroy all mankind with a continual flood of evil, it is also true that God will never turn us over to the will of the devil. He has promised to deliver us and give us victory over all the works of the evil one. While God has provided many means by which we may receive His help in times of need, nothing is of greater importance than intercessory prayer. As intercessors in our day take their place alongside the intercessors of all ages, God will move in our generation in a mighty way.

While interceding before the throne of God, our minds will often drift from local needs to some other part of the world, because the Holy Spirit is praying through us to birth revival there, even though we may know little, or nothing, about that land.

Nigeria, Africa

Years ago during times of intercessory prayer my mind would go again and again to the nation of Nigeria, Africa. Frequently, in my mind's eye, I would see tens of thousands of Nigerians coming to the Lord. Sometimes I could see the face of a man for whom the Spirit of God was interceding, as He sought to bring forth a strong leader for revival in Nigeria. Years later, I met the man I had seen during prayer, Doctor Benson Idahosa, who pastors Miracle Center in Benin City, Nigeria. Over a million people have come to Christ in Nigeria in recent years under Doctor Idahosa's ministry.

Intercessory prayer has always been a major factor in the spreading of God's kingdom to all the nations of earth. In Old Testament days, God placed the people of Israel as a nation of intercessors among the nations of the world. As God chose Israel to be intercessors for all other nations, so He is still calling His people today to join the ranks of intercessors and stand in the gap for a lost and dying world.

God first draws us to the place of prayer by His Holy Spirit. Then, after gaining our cooperation as prayer warriors, the Holy Spirit begins to prepare us for revival and a new move of God that will bring healing and salvation to the nations.

Intercessors and Prophets

The Bible clearly shows that the healing of a nation comes through the combined ministries of intercessors and prophets. The record of God's frequent intervention in the affairs of Israel reveals that, always, after the intercessors had prevailed, God raised up a prophet.

Joseph

First, there was Joseph, whose prophetic ministry was birthed through earnest prayer during times of great personal trials. Truly, through his ministry, healing came to both Israel and Egypt — the just and the unjust. The revival in Joseph's day came none too soon for the millions who were facing death at the hand of a worldwide famine. The results of this mighty revival lingered for many generations during which Israel and Egypt dwelt together in peace and prosperity.

Several principles can be drawn from Joseph's life.

➤ Hard times bring some men to their knees in prayer.

➤ Prayer can birth prophetic ministries.

➤ God's mercy and power fall upon the just and unjust alike.

➤ Hopeless world conditions are subject to change and often conquered as God's power and mercy are demonstrated among the nations.

➤ Long times of peace follow times of great revival.

Moses

Many years after Joseph's death, a pharaoh arose to the throne of Egypt who did not understand how God had worked through Joseph, and he brought the people of Israel into bondage. Again, the people of Israel prayed earnestly, crying out to God for deliverance from the oppressive living and working conditions that the new pharaoh put upon them. God heard their prayers, and He raised up Moses with another prophetic-revival ministry. As the Spirit of God moved upon Moses, the nation of Israel was stirred by a new revival of faith in God.

Even though Israel had maintained their outward appearance as a religious people while they were in Egypt, at the same time they had become so entangled in the fleshly systems of Egypt that they lost the glory of God. Through revival power, accompanied by signs, wonders and miracles, the reality of the glory of God was restored to the people. As a result many nations were touched with a fresh witness that the God of Israel was a God of power and mercy; indeed,

He was a faithful deliverer who was able to fulfill His word, keep His covenants, and maintain a reasonable and orderly timetable to accomplish His purposes in the earth.

Joshua

After the death of Moses, Joshua, a man of deep prayer, was raised up and, through his ministry, God took His people one step further in His plan to send revival throughout the earth. Although Moses was used to establish Israel in the blood covenant and, over a period of forty years, delivered them from everything that had kept them out of their land of inheritance, it took a new wave of God's power moving in a new generation to bring them into possession of that land.

Through Joshua's ministry, God not only took them into the land, but also gave them a testimony to share with the nations. Israel would now say among the nations, "He who brought us out has also brought us in, and He can do the same for you," Deuteronomy 6:23; I Corinthians 10:11. The revival in Joshua's day brought the people into a land flowing with milk and honey; a land of mountains and valleys, wherein were the treasures of gold, silver, brass, iron and oil; a land of orchards, pastures, vineyards and cities. The people literally moved into a land prepared for them, a place where they could live in God's presence and enjoy such an abundant life that all the nations of the earth would not only call them blessed, but they would also call upon the Lord and be saved.

God's promise to give Israel the land of Canaan was an important part of His plan to save the world. Not only had He given them the land as their home, it was also to be the base from which they could let the light of His glory shine throughout the earth.

Samuel

As the years passed, the children of Israel drifted further and further from the purpose for which God had brought them into the promised land. The light of God was growing dim in their midst and they were losing the battle against sin and wickedness. As in all times of apostasy, there was a remnant who continued to believe God and who continued to intercede before the throne of God night and day.

Hannah, who would later become the mother of Samuel, was among those intercessors.

Hannah's sorrow and distress at not being able to have a child, drove her to the place of prayer where she poured out her bitter complaint to the Lord. Hannah vowed to God that if He would give her a son, she would give him to the Lord. Hannah's prayer was answered, and she gave birth to Samuel whose prophetic ministry brought healing to the land and turned the people back to God. This is a beautiful example of how God will use the desires of our hearts to accomplish the desires and purposes of His heart. Hannah wanted a son; God wanted a man whom He could use to turn Israel back to Himself. Samuel was the fulfillment of both of those desires.

During Samuel's ministry, Israel was being prepared to grasp the idea that God's kingdom on earth would rule among all nations. (See Chapter 5, "Revival in the Year of Jubilee.") Israel's first thought, however, was to establish their own kingdom. To fulfill their idea about the new kingdom, they chose Saul as king. Saul's carnal ways temporarily hindered revival as he walked in the pride of the flesh, seeking to establish his own rule and his own will as the authority of the kingdom and ignoring the will of God for His kingdom among men. When God's will is followed, revival is experienced. When man's will is followed, revival is hindered. But, in spite of Saul's refusal to follow God's will, Samuel and others continued in intercessory prayer, refusing to give up hope for the complete work of revival and restoration in their nation.

Out of this intercessory prayer, the ministry of David was birthed. Again we see God adding a new dimension to the work of revival in a new generation of believers.

David

David's entire life is an illustration of how intercessory prayer opens heaven's gates and prepares men to prevail over their enemies. From one situation to another, David prevailed as time after time he sought the Lord's help. By the end of David's life, he was able to deliver to Solomon, and to all generations that would follow after him, a strong example of how revival is possible in every generation.

During Solomon's reign, Israel truly became the people through whom God's glory shone forth as a light to the surrounding nations.

Years later, Ahab and Jezebel sat on the throne of David in Jerusalem, but they did not follow David's ways. They turned from God's will and followed Saul's example of self-will. As a result, great darkness fell on the land. The false prophets of Baal, who promoted immorality and fleshly living were the popular people of that day. During this time of great darkness, idol worshiping and backsliding, many intercessors were hidden in the caves of Israel praying for revival while living on bread and water.

Elijah

Through their intercessory prayers, God raised up the prophet Elijah. Revival power began to increase, and the ground swell of spiritual life in Israel rose to the point that Elijah was able to not only confront and slay four hundred prophets of Baal who promoted an antichrist lifestyle, but he also confronted the wicked ungodly rulers, Ahab and Jezebel.

In the ministry of Elijah, God began to make known that the throne of revival upon which David had sat was not a natural throne. Elijah never came to the natural throne in Jerusalem, but throughout his lifetime he ministered from the spiritual throne of David in kingdom authority.

The throne of revival is always restored when intercessors have prevailed as did the seven thousand in Elijah's day. Of the seven thousand, God said, "These have never bowed their knee to Baal." God, Himself, laid claim to the seven thousand as equal servants to Elijah in their role as part of the army that was bringing revival. Elijah's short prayer on Mount Carmel brought the fire on the sacrifice, but it was the years of intercessory prayer of the seven thousand that brought revival fire on all of Israel.

Elisha

The story of Elisha, who received Elijah's mantle and a double portion of Elijah's ministry and anointing, illustrates further that the authority and power of the throne of revival is vested in the anointing of the Spirit and not in a natural throne.

All intercessors should realize that while God will answer their prayers and send prophetic-revival ministries, generally these ministries will not sit as the heads of organizations and denominations. While most leaders of denominations are good administrators and public relations people, seldom do they excel in the prophetic ministry. Even though some organizations have been centers of revival movements in the past, the authority and power of revival is not passed on in the natural succession of earthly position. The authority and power of revival is found in a fresh anointing of the Holy Spirit. This fresh anointing is available to all who continue in intercessory prayer.

Jonah

The prophetic ministry of Jonah was birthed in a most unique prayer chamber. Through earnest prayer, Jonah was delivered from the belly of the great fish. Then through earnest prayer, the entire city of Nineveh and the nation of Syria were saved from divine punishment in that generation.

Jonah's experience in the belly of the great fish illustrates the condition of nations that are sinking in the mire of total rebellion and strangling in great sinfulness. Like Jonah, these nations are running from God and appear to be going down for the last time. Two hope-giving facts are learned from this story. We need not cast away our faith concerning a generation of Christians who, like Jonah, refuse to do God's will. Neither should we give up on a generation of people, like those in the city of Nineveh, who appear to be destined for divine punishment. Jonah's story illustrates God's ability to bring correction and redirection to His people as well as repentance and salvation to the unsaved.

Daniel

In Daniel's day, though there was neither a throne nor a king in Jerusalem, some of the people who had been taken captive to Babylon were again learning the power of intercessory prayer. Chief among these was Daniel. So once more a new wave of revival swept in upon God's people. However, this revival did not come upon the people who remained in Jerusalem; it came upon the people of God who had been scattered to other nations. This shows us that revival can take place anywhere in the world when there are intercessors. Revival does not come to a people just because they belong to the so-called "right church"; it comes because there are intercessors in their midst who will not give up and who continue to seek God night and day. Intercessors of our day would do well to echo the prayer of Daniel 9.

Haggai, Zechariah, Ezra and Nehemiah

In the years following the intercession of Daniel and others in exile in Babylon, there arose several prophetic ministries. Among them were the ministries of Haggai, Zechariah, Ezra and Nehemiah. These men, each in divine timing, appeared on the scene with such revival power that not only was the city of Jerusalem and the temple rebuilt, but the people were delivered from their sinful ways and kingdom order was restored in Israel.

Intercessory prayer does give birth to prophetic ministries and these ministries do bring revival. This principle is repeated so often in Scripture that we can expect God to work this way anytime intercessors continually seek His face.

What if there are no Intercessors?

Now the question must be asked: What can we expect or what hope do we have when there are no intercessors? To find the answer, we need only go to Isaiah 59 and take a closer look at the real message in the chapter.

The first portion of Isaiah 59 presents the picture of the hopelessness of men as they sink into the pit of sin and shame. This picture could apply to any generation when men forsake God's Word and turn to their own ways.

The increase of evil should never be seen as a sign that God has turned man over to the devil and has refused to intervene in his struggle with sin. The increase of evil in any generation merely illustrates, among other things, the great need for intercessors.

God has promised that even during times when evil abounds and the enemy rushes in like a flood, the Spirit of the Lord will raise up a standard against him and the nations will fear the Lord, Isaiah 59:19.

Yet in Isaiah's day, the Lord found no intercessors to stand in the gap, make up the hedge, and turn away destruction from the land. All Israel should have been aware of the many times they had been saved in their past from the wrath of man and God as intercessors obtained mercy and help in the times of need. Many intercessors should have daily filled the house of God. Yet there were none — not even the prophet Isaiah.

➤ Would God let His plan for that generation fail because there were no intercessors? No.

➤ Could God's mercy be blocked because of man's failure? No.

God's love, then and now, will always find a way to help man, even though man has utterly failed. How did God find a way to compensate for a lack of intercessors?

The Lord, Himself, became the great intercessor and stood in the gap. His right arm brought salvation, Isaiah 59:16. Jesus is the eternal prophet, priest and king, and, as such, he is the great intercessor who cannot fail. He is the one who always sits on the throne of glory. We have a high priest who ever lives to make intercession for us. Hebrews 7:25.

When God can find no intercessors, Jesus will sovereignly move on our behalf. Therefore, whether there are many intercessors, few intercessors or no intercessors, Jesus remains the eternal great intercessor. In each generation we can expect that sooner or later God will make His mercy and power known and new prophetic-revival ministries will rekindle the fires of revival in the earth. Malachi further substantiates our hope in God's everlasting mercy and His eternal willingness to intercede on our behalf as he declared God's word:

> *"For I am the Lord, I change not; therefore ye sons of Jacob are not consumed,"* Malachi 3:6.

We do not suggest that Christians give up intercessory prayer, knowing that sooner or later the Lord will move anyway. We are rather saying that we should not become overly concerned to the point of discouragement by those who will not join us in intercessory prayer since we know that the Lord, Himself, is our intercessory prayer partner. One intercessor and the Lord are a majority.

When we understand Jesus' role as the great intercessor, we will neither be discouraged at a lack of intercessors, nor will we believe that any nation is without hope. The intercessory ministry of Christ is for all people of all nations and all generations.

God's promise that He, Himself, will be our great and eternal intercessor, is sealed with these words:

> "...*My Spirit* [the spirit of grace] *that is upon thee* [Isaiah] *and my words* [words of mercy] *which I have put in thy mouth, shall not depart out of thy mouth, nor out of the mouth of thy seed, nor out of the mouth of thy seed's seed, saith the Lord, from henceforth and for ever,*" Isaiah 59:21.

Our hope for revival is rooted deeply in God's unchangeable nature and His infallible Word.

In His role of great intercessor, Christ will do three things for us in enforcing God's plan of recurring revival:

> ➤ He will pray for us to join Him and encourage us in intercessory prayer so that man's great needs might be met.

> ➤ When we fail to pray for all things to be restored, He will pick up our lack and be the surety of those better promises that speak of total restoration and revival.

> ➤ When there are no intercessors at all, He will make up the full lack. He will stand in the gap and obtain from the Father a fresh outpouring of the Spirit upon all flesh. God has promised that even in wrath, He will remember mercy and He will always revive His work in the midst of the years, Habakkuk 3:2.

Since nothing is impossible with God, or with those who believe and trust in Him, we can expect revival and healing of the nations in our generation. Believers of all nations must be ready to answer the heavenly call to enter the intercessory prayer chamber and seek God until His Spirit is poured out upon all flesh and revival sweeps through all lands again and again.

Questions for this chapter on page 215

I do verily believe that when God shall accomplish it [unity], it will be the effect of love, and not the cause of love. It will proceed from love, before it brings forth love.

John Owen, Puritan

What cannot warrant a breach where there is union, that cannot warrantably be the ground to keep up a division.

James Durham, 17th Century Puritan

Take away union and there can be no communion.

John Flavel, Puritan

Communication is the secret to unity. If people will talk to one another, barriers will come down. How many pastors ever invite a pastor of another denomination to their home for fellowship? How many people pray for the church of a different denomination down the street? It's awfully hard to be at enmity with anybody when you start praying for them.

Freda Lindsay, Christ for the Nations Institute,
Miracle Living Magazine, 1982

Chapter 12

UNITY

We must first be in union with God before we can be in unity with others. Unity with God creates a God-consciousness, and this awareness of God's presence gives us an extra desire to put natural things aside so that nothing will hinder our fellowship with God or with His people. Years ago a song writer was moved to pen a verse that says it so well:

> "Nothing between my soul and the Savior so that His blessed face may be seen. Nothing preventing the least of His favors; keep the way clear, let nothing between."

When we continue to keep our relationship with God a top priority in our daily walk, nothing will hide our view of His face. Then the fire of His presence will burn in our hearts in the same fashion as the fire of the Eternal Father burns in Christ our Lord. Unity flows out of the believer who is hid with Christ in God.

Christ's Prayer for Unity

Revival is the very nature of God working in and through His people to such a degree that the same power working within will also be manifested to the world as they see that believers have love for one another. In Christ's prayer that we might all be one, He prayed for us to be made perfect (mature and complete) in unity, so that all men would know that we are His disciples and the world would believe that the Father had sent the Son, John 17. That prayer has been answered in many ways:

- ➤ His prayer was first answered in His death, for when He died, we all died with Him, II Corinthians 5:14.

- ➤ His prayer was also answered in the sanctifying power of His death. He that sanctifies and they who are sanctified are all of one, Hebrews 2:11.

- ➤ We are also made one in the Spirit because we who are Christ's have been raised up together with Him in resurrection power and we are seated together with Him in heavenly places, Ephesians 2:6.

- ➤ We are one because there is one Body, one Spirit, one Lord, one faith, one baptism, and one God and Father of all, Ephesians 4:4-6.

- ➤ Finally, we remain one in the Spirit because Christ cannot be divided, I Corinthians 1:13.

Thus, the direction of our efforts to keep the unity of the Spirit working mightily in us is first Godward. Our efforts should not be in persuading others to agree with us. We must first agree with God, for He is the author of our unity. As we hold fast to this good confession, God will continue to work His great work of unity in us, and the blessings of new life will keep revival spreading through us to others.

Unity is first a fact of truth in the Spirit. We see an example of this with Israel of whom it is said: They all drank of that same spiritual drink, which was Christ, I Corinthians 10:4. Our unity as believers is an accomplished fact from the day we first placed our faith in Christ as Savior and are born into the family of God. We thereafter must learn to endeavor to keep that unity.

> *"Endeavoring to keep the unity of the Spirit in the bond of peace,"* Ephesians 4:3.

For example, though a husband and wife are one flesh according to the Bible, yet they may not dwell together in unity. When they do not, they miss the blessings and benefits of unity that should be theirs.

In order to appreciate the great need for unity, let us remember that God said even of Adam, who had a perfect relationship with God, "It is not good for man to be alone." Man alone has a limited experience with God, but together with others, we experience an increased revelation of God.

Benefits of unity

Some of the increased blessings and benefits resulting from unity among God's people are seen in Psalm 133.

> *"Behold, how good and how pleasant it is for brethren to dwell together in unity! It is like the precious ointment upon the head, that ran down upon the beard, even Aaron's beard: that went down to the skirts of his garments; as the dew of Hermon, and as the dew that descended upon the mountains of Zion: for there the Lord commanded the blessing, even life for evermore."*

This Psalm shows us that God has commanded blessing where brethren dwell together in unity. This blessing is the life and fiery presence of the Lord manifested in the midst of His people — and this is truly revival!

The blessings promised in Psalm 133 are conditional, for there must first be unity among God's people before there can be the blessings. When we consider man's nature, we realize that the unity required must be a unity in the Spirit, which is a work of God in our lives, not a work of human energy.

Anointing

Not only does unity release abundant life in rivers of blessing, it also brings a special anointing. The *"precious ointment"* spoken of in Psalm 133:2, which covered Aaron, is symbolic of a ministry saturated with the anointing. When Jesus read from Isaiah 61 as He stood in the synagogue of Nazareth, He was walking in the saturation anointing of Psalm 133.

> *"The Spirit of the Lord is upon me, because he hath anointed me to preach the gospel to the poor; he hath sent me to heal the brokenhearted, to preach deliverance to the captives, and recovering of sight to the blind, to set at liberty them that are bruised, to preach the acceptable year of the Lord,"* Luke 4:18,19.

Jesus' ministry following His declaration in Luke 4 caused revival to erupt everywhere He went. And ultimately the apostles, maintaining the unity and walking in that same anointing, spread revival throughout the nations in that generation.

Another example showing how unity among God's people releases the flow of the anointing is seen in Zechariah 4. Here we read of the two olive trees, one on either side of the candlestick with a bowl of oil. According to verses 12 through 14 of this chapter, these two olive trees represent the anointed ones who stand beside the Lord in His ministry throughout the whole earth. This shows how the oil of the Spirit flows through us when we dwell together in unity. For true believers in Jesus Christ are the anointed ones who labor together with the Lord to bring the gospel message to the ends of the earth. The candlestick is the source of light in the temple of the Lord, which gives light for the service of the altar and also becomes as a beacon light shining out to the lost and dying, showing them the way to the altar. The lesson is so very clearly taught throughout the Scriptures: Where two or more gather together in one accord, Jesus will be working in power.

David's example

An example of how increasing unity brings increasing anointing and ultimate victory is seen in the life of David. In David's first anointing, when he was yet a young shepherd boy, he was brought into union with the prophets and the anointed leaders, including King Saul, I Samuel 16:13. David retained unity of the Spirit with Saul although Saul, himself, later turned aside. David refused to break the unity of the Spirit by becoming disrespectful and hostile toward a fallen leader. Through that anointing Goliath was defeated and the many attacks of Saul were endured by David as he was learning the lessons necessary to prepare him to be king.

In David's second anointing, as he was anointed king over the house of Judah, he was united with the people of Judah, II Samuel 2:4. Through this event, more and more brethren of like mind joined David's ranks, and increased unity brought increased anointing; thus, it follows that the results of David's ministry increased by the same measure. At this time David and his co-workers were able to do that which neither Joshua nor those who went before David had been able to accomplish. By this increased anointing they were able to go up to the heights of Zion and subdue the Jebusites who had fiercely held this most treasured spot in the kingdom. Later Solomon built the temple in this choice spot, and from that day the call has gone forth to the ends of the earth: Come up to the Lord who dwells in the heights of Zion.

Finally, David's third anointing came as all Israel was united under his kingship, II Samuel 5:3. Through this total-unity anointing, wars ceased in all Israel's borders and righteousness and praise were established in Zion. For through this ultimate anointing and unity, David was able to receive from the hand of the Lord the pattern by which Solomon later built the temple.

The hope of worldwide, continuous revival for our generation rests in the hope of total unity among God's people. As that day of total unity draws near, the divine plan for building up the house of the Lord in all nations will come to us as surely as God's plan came to David for that first temple in Zion. And as it was in that day, so it will be in ours: The knowledge of the glory of the Lord will go out into all the earth.

Anointed teaching and doctrine

Psalm 133 holds yet another blessing for those who dwell in unity. This blessing is equally important to revival, for it is the blessing contained in the dew that comes down upon Mount Hermon. The "dew of Hermon" is symbolic of anointed teaching and doctrine.

> *"My doctrine shall drop as the rain, my speech shall distil as the dew...,"* **Deuteronomy 32:2.**

Hermon means "the place of devotion," which speaks of a completely consecrated life and a singleness of mind unto the Lord. No revival will continue, much less spread, without strong anointed teaching and doctrine.

What a picture of spreading revival we see in Psalm 133! Brethren dwelling together in unity, the life of God flowing from His throne, the oil of anointing flowing upon His servants, and the teachings and doctrines coming down as dew saturating every blade of grass in the field.

No generation gap

Jeremiah prophesied that in times of restoration there would be a surge of unity as multitudes returned from backsliding and walking in their own ways. He said the old man, the young man, and the virgin would all come together in one accord unto the goodness of the Lord. Here we see that the generation-gap is swallowed up in the restoration work of the Spirit as young and old alike return to the heights of Zion. Jeremiah also predicts that as unity increases, sorrow and mourning will flee away and joy and rejoicing will be the order of the day.

> *"Therefore they shall come and sing in the height of Zion, and shall flow together to the goodness of the Lord, for wheat, and for wine, and for oil, and for the young of the flock and of the herd: and their soul shall be as a watered garden; and they shall not sorrow any more at all. Then shall the virgin rejoice in the dance, both young men and old together: for I will turn their mourning into joy, and will comfort them, and make them rejoice from their sorrow,"* **Jeremiah 31:12,13.**

Revival spreads

The prophet Micah gives us another example of how unity among God's people causes revival to spread. In Micah 4:1-4 we read that the mountain of the Lord's house shall be established above all other mountains. Often when the Scriptures speak of mountains they are speaking symbolically of the high place where God's ways are firm and established. When God's people are established in the "high place" of unity, we will see Micah's prophecy fulfilled again.

Micah said that many nations, even strong nations afar off, would come and say, "Teach us your ways." He said that the word of the Lord would go forth in such power from the exalted house of the Lord that even though the people were from many different backgrounds they would all learn God's way of peace and unity. In that place swords would be turned into plowshares and spears into pruning hooks. The power of a united people working together to let God have His way draws people to Christ even as iron is drawn to a magnet.

Love among believers

The power that draws nonbelievers to Christ, according to John 13:35, is that they see the love believers have for one another. The greater the love, the greater the drawing power.

What a wonderful hope we have! We have the hope of the Spirit of God working in each believer and working through each believer to strengthen one another. Ephesians 4 not only tells us to endeavor to keep the unity, but also declares that as each member supplies the need one of another, the body will make increase of itself in love. To me, this is true revival. For when the body makes increase of itself in love, the true testimony of Jesus Christ is seen working in a practical way among His people.

Know Christ

The apostle Paul understood one of the most important keys to keeping the unity of the Spirit.

"I am determined not to know anything among you, save Jesus Christ, and him crucified," I Corinthians 2:2

Paul's determination to know nothing among the churches except Jesus Christ and Him crucified was based on the fact that when Christ was crucified, our sins and all that is against us were nailed with Him to the cross, Colossians 2:14, 15. Thus, all division and difference among God's people are, by faith, nailed to the cross. Paul therefore boldly said, "Christ is not divided," I Corinthians 1:13. Yes, in the flesh there will always be difference of opinions that can lead to division. But when we understand that all who are in Christ have become new creations in the Spirit, we will not judge men after the flesh anymore.

Christ works in all believers

Next, we see that we can keep the unity of the Spirit by acknowledging God's mighty power working in every believer. When our eyes are trained through faith to see that Christ is always at work in our brothers, we will find it easier to keep the unity of the Spirit in the bond of peace, Ephesians 4:3. If we look for fault in others, we will always find them; however, if we look for the work of faith in the Spirit, that we will always find. For God is always at work in all saints and in all churches reconciling all things unto Himself.

Paul also said that his hope and the rule of his ministry was that by one person's faith increasing, the faith of others would also be increased abundantly, II Corinthians 10:13-18. This mutual increase in faith always results in the gospel being preached more than before. Again, we see how unity is the fuel that spreads revival.

Unity among watchmen

Isaiah 52:7-9 gives us a further picture of unity among brethren. There we read of unity among the watchmen. These watchmen, according to Isaiah, are those who proclaim peace and salvation and who bring glad tidings. When the watchmen see eye to eye and with one mind lift up their voices together and sing the same song, "Our God reigns", there will be revival.

Revival will not spread when some watchmen say that the Lord *will reign* in the future, but sin and evil *are reigning* now. Times of sweeping revivals occur when all the watchmen have the same message as declared by the prophet Isaiah:

"The Lord hath made bare His holy arm [revealed His power] *in the eyes of all the nations; and all the ends of the earth shall see the salvation of our God,"* Isaiah 52:10

Unity is like a diamond that stands out above all other jewels, reflecting many facets of the light. Nothing could glorify God more than the orderly transfer of revival from one generation to another. The song of both the young prophets and the old should be that God will send revival again and again. The old men, when telling the young men of God's mighty works in the past, should never imply that God will not move in such a way again. Neither should the young men boast that they have something so much greater that the old men will be ashamed. When we walk in love and unity there will be no place for proud boasting and competition.

Fathers' hearts turned to the children

Malachi's prophecy says that God will send the same spirit that was upon Elijah the prophet, and the hearts of the fathers will be turned to the children and the hearts of the children to the fathers, Malachi 4. Truly God's plan is for revival to spread from one generation to another in the same manner in which the anointing and revival spread from Elijah's generation to Elisha's. Elisha took the mantle of Elijah and went on to do double the works of Elijah and spread the revival into regions beyond that of Elijah's day. Yet he did so without conflict or competition with Elijah. No wonder God promised to send anointed ministries like Elijah's again and again.

David and Solomon

This principle of the hearts of children and fathers flowing together is also found with David and Solomon. David had other sons who did not allow their hearts to be turned to their father. The most outstanding example was Absalom. He yearned to have David's glory, but was not willing to walk in his steps. Absalom sought for greatness without his father, and his disloyalty and disunity caused the revival flow of David's time to be temporarily halted, and for a season Absalom kept the kingdom in confusion. Thus Absalom's lack of unity with the work of God in the previous generation caused him to lose out on the good thing Solomon later enjoyed.

Doctor Charles Price

We have seen similar lack of unity in our century. Doctor Charles Price, who was a father of revival in the early part of this century, gave a word just before his passing that was much like the word Paul gave to the churches of his day. Paul said that after his departure, grievous wolves would enter in, not sparing the flock of God, Acts 20:29. Likewise, Doctor Price said that after his death there would be a time in which well-meaning ministries would turn from the way of the Lord and would put a price tag on the gospel with their emphasis on raising money. And while it would appear to many as though these ministries would bring another great revival, merchandising of the things of God would only bring more confusion among the rank and file of believers. His prophecy also said that these practices would come to an end during the time of another sweeping revival that would take place in the last part of the 20th Century. Thank God!

Almost forty years have passed since Doctor Price's death, and it is time for the Elijah-type ministries to turn the hearts of the children to the fathers. We are the children, and the fathers are those who experienced great revivals in past generations. Doctor Price, Smith Wigglesworth and others prophesied that the greatest revival in history would come at the close of this century. We who seek that God's will be done in our lifetime must also allow our hearts to be united with the hearts of the revival leaders of past generations. For without us, they cannot be made complete, just as David without Solomon could not see the vision of the Lord fulfilled.

When Solomon's heart was turned to that of his father, David, there was more to be considered than the ambitious desires of a young man grasping for riches and position. The true desire of Solomon's heart is seen in his prayer at the dedication of the temple, as he asked God to verify and fulfill in his generation the word given to his father, David, I Kings 8:26. Solomon's concept of unity was more than an occasional reference as to how God had used his father. His concept of unity was to walk wholly in all the ways of his father.

The glory of Solomon's kingdom is testified to throughout the Scriptures and was known throughout the whole earth. The widespread effect of the unity of purpose in following God's ways, shown in the lives of David and Solomon, is seen in I Kings 10:4-9. Here, we read that the Queen of Sheba came to see if the fame concerning Solomon's great wisdom and the reputation of His God was all that she had heard. Upon seeing all that God had established in Solomon's kingdom, she said, *"It was a true report that I heard...Howbeit...the half was not told me...."*

We can see that revival spread from David's house to Solomon's, throughout the house of Israel, and unto the ends of the earth. Solomon's wisdom is seen in that he walked in all the statutes of his father, David, I Kings 3:3. His wisdom is also seen in his ability to teach others; all of his servants were taught to walk in that same wisdom. Just as the fame and wisdom of Solomon was spread abroad in his day, so in our day, all the earth will see the glory of God when His servants walk in the wisdom of Solomon.

Although the natural circumstances of society are different in our time, yet the principles of unity remain the same. It is time for every believer to stand up like a watchman on the wall and endeavor to keep the unity of the Spirit. To talk about worldwide unity among believers is not enough; unity starts with the brother who is nearest at hand.

When we continue to pray that we may personally walk in unity with those around us, the Holy Spirit will shed the love of God abroad in our hearts to such a degree that unity among the brethren will be spontaneous and continuous. Revival will then be carried like the waves of the sea with the rising tide, covering more and more of the untouched areas of the earth.

Questions for this chapter on page 217

Patterns of spiritual renewal . . . an individual or small group of God's people becomes conscious of their sins and backslidden condition, and vows to forsake all that is displeasing to God. . . a leader or leaders arise with prophetic insights into the causes and remedies of the problems, and a new awareness of the holy and pure character of the Lord is present. . . . many understand and take part in a higher spiritual life. . . widespread renewal that includes the simultaneous conversion of many people to Christ.

Christian History

The blessings offered in the covenant made with Abraham are ours. A vital part of that covenant is the promise that the church would be a blessing to all nations. . . It should fill our hearts with hope and thankfulness that through Christ and His church all nations without exception will be blessed.

J. Marcellus Kik, *An Eschatology of Victory*

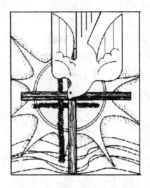

Chapter 13

LET'S MOVE ON WITH GOD

Believers everywhere are saying, "Let's move on with God." Throughout the Body of Christ, many are filled with the fresh expectation of another great spiritual awakening. Excitement abounds on every hand like that which surrounds the preparation for a journey. Signs are appearing in the Body of Christ worldwide that God's people are on the verge of another major display of His miracle-working power.

We can compare this to the time when the children of Israel crossed over the Jordan River. In my understanding of the Scriptures, the river Jordan frequently symbolizes the river of God — a place that must be crossed in order to enter into the better things God has prepared for us. And today, the Spirit of God is urging us to cross over into the harvest of a new and mighty revival.

What does this crossing over mean to us as individuals, as local fellowships, and as the Body of Christ worldwide? Can we move on into a new wave of revival without a time of preparation? What kind of preparation is necessary for the Church of this generation to reach new heights and new depths of God's grace so that we can reap the harvest at hand and fulfill God's plan? In the third chapter of Joshua, we learn through the example of Israel's crossing Jordan what we can expect in this generation.

Our story of Joshua and the children of Israel opens in Joshua 3:1 as the children of Israel left their place of encampment and came to the banks of the Jordan River where they lodged for three days.

Resting in Faith

To lodge beside the river of God speaks to us of coming to rest in our circumstances, knowing that God is at work preparing a way for us to cross over through His miracle-working power. The three days the children of Israel waited also holds significance for us. Three days, in Bible symbolism, represents the time required to perfect a work. Jesus was in the heart of the earth for three days to perfect His work of redemption.

The children of Israel were in a place where they could do nothing but rest in faith, knowing God was working on their behalf. The promised land, with all its provisions and possibilities, lay before them, but they could only enter in when they were ready to follow the leading of God into new areas of faith.

At that time Joshua told the people to sanctify themselves for the Lord was going to do wonders among them, Joshua 3:5. God had a unique method by which He planned to take the children of Israel across the Jordan, but they had to be prepared for what He was going to do.

Many of us have prayed for revival to sweep through the nations of the world, and we believe that God will sovereignly intervene in great miracle-working power in our day. However, just as Israel had to be prepared for the miraculous parting of the waters, so we must be prepared to do our part to receive God's wonders and miracles. Many times this preparation time comes as God allows us to be enclosed by adverse circumstances which require that we grow in faith.

Greater things to come

While in a position of waiting, we may appear to be at a standstill and feel weak and unable to go on; however, in reality, we are being prepared for greater things to come.

As we become settled in the place of resting and waiting, we will be prepared in the following areas of faith:

- ➤ First, our faith will be increased to see that there is a way where no way appears.
- ➤ Second, we will see how to move on and take advantage of the possibilities on the other side.
- ➤ Third, as our faith increases we will receive an unusual awareness of God's timings so that we will neither move ahead of God nor lag behind Him.

When the time of preparation has produced the needed growth to move in step-by-step timing with God, we can then expect to cross the river into the good things that God has prepared for us. We will experience revival to the degree we are prepared to move on with God. He is willing to lead. We must be prepared to follow.

God is patient

Waiting is difficult. When we are on a journey, we do not like traffic holdups. We are always in a hurry to get to our destination. However, God is never in a hurry. He is always patiently working in us and changing us while we are on our journeys. Much of the needed change in our hearts and attitudes takes place during the waiting times.

All of life is a journey. We set goals, we look for opportunities, and we head for open doors. However, the reaching of our goals is secondary with God. His primary objective is that when we get to the end of our journeys, we will not be the same as when we started, but we will have been changed into the image of His Son.

Progress in the Christian life is measured in segments of growing from faith to faith and from glory to glory. In each of these segments of growth, we will be brought to a place where the Spirit of God deals with us and seeks to free us from more of the self-life and reveal more of the Christ-life in us. It takes both the preparation in our hearts and the miracles from God's hand to move on with God.

Preparation

Many believers want revival without preparation. But vessels lacking the tempering gained through the waiting period will crumble under the pressures placed on them during times of God's reaping the harvest.

When God speaks to us of a new place, a promised land, or a new wave of revival, we are usually enjoying a mountaintop experience. At that point, looking across to the "land" He has promised, about all we can see is that the new place is beautiful and blessed. Faith rises and we often become excited in hope, expecting God to do great things. We say, "Praise God! that's where I'm going," and we move out in the measure of faith we possess at that time. However, a major difficulty soon appears. We discover that to move into the new land of promise we must go through the river of God again, where once more elements of the self-life are challenged and more of the Christ-life is released.

Moving into a new realm in God can be difficult. We are creatures of habit and become comfortable and secure in familiar principles and do not want to leave them for unknown and untried ways.

Learning new faith principles

As we move on in our journey of faith, we will be brought many times to the place where faith principles that brought us through in the past are not sufficient. Perhaps in times past we have gone to God in prayer, making known our needs and we have experienced His delivering power again and again. But then one day we find ourselves in a situation where prayer is not enough. It may be time for us to learn about the power of praise. And so now we hear the Lord say, "Give thanks and praise me in this circumstance."

We say, "Lord, I don't see anything in this for which to praise you. Just get me out of this situation." But as we rest in faith beside the river, we will eventually learn the value of new principles and become willing to move on with God.

During these resting and waiting periods, God not only prepares us for crossing over, but He also grooms and equips us for the good things waiting for us on the other side. It is not uncommon to be led of the Holy Spirit into a new place only to find on our arrival that we are facing greater obstacles. Many members of our congregation have moved to Phoenix as the Spirit of God led them. They came expecting everything to fall into place, but upon their arrival they found many obstacles. But the fact that they encountered obstacles did not mean the leading was wrong; the obstacles caused them to press into God for more of His wisdom and truth.

Personal example

My wife and I faced the same learning process when we moved to Phoenix. Over and over the Lord confirmed that the move was of Him. But when we arrived in Phoenix we found that a large company had moved hundreds of workers into the city two months earlier and most of the rentals were taken. We stayed in motels for weeks. Finally we found a house, and although it was better than the motel, it was not what I had in mind. Before we moved to Phoenix, the Lord had shown me a vision of a lovely house in which we would live. The house we found at first had no resemblance to the one I had seen in the vision. As it turned out, the house in the vision had not been built at that time. We had to wait eight years to see that word of the Lord fulfilled.

During those years of waiting, I did not know that we were experiencing the divine process of learning the faith rest. What a principle! Now I understand how this principle always gives us the upper hand and helps us to receive God's best for our lives.

Stand still

When we have learned to wait on God and rest in hope, we are ready for the next step. We are ready to step out in faith into the waters where the Holy Spirit is moving.

In our story of Joshua and the children of Israel, the priests who bore the ark of the covenant were commanded to stand still as soon as their feet were in the water, Joshua 3:8. Once we have taken our first step at the command of the Lord, we are then to stand still in the river of the Spirit. See Ezekiel 47. While we stand still in the river, it is a time set aside by God where the flow of the Spirit stops our human reasoning, harnesses our human zeal, and silences our human emotions. To stand still is to say, "Here I am, Lord, with my feet in the river of God and revival power flowing through my life, knowing fully that I can only take the next step as you lead the way, for in my own strength I can do nothing."

Often times when we are standing still in the river of God, people will come to us and ask us what we are going to do next. The only reply we can make at such times is that we are going to stand still in obedience and by faith practice the good things God has already taught us until He shows us the next move, Philippians 3:16.

Personal example

When we first moved to Phoenix and pastored a small congregation, I was in the place of standing still by faith with my feet in the river of God waiting to see my ministry open up and be fruitful as God had promised.

My experience was much like that of Ezekiel. God first measured out a thousand cubits and there Ezekiel stood, receiving the blessings of the first measurement of revival. The important thing was not how soon the Lord would measure out another thousand cubits and take him deeper into the river. The important thing was that all the time Ezekiel was standing there waiting on God, the river was continuing to flow through his life.

For five years I waited for God to reveal the next step. As I stood in the river of God, I felt its waters flowing all around me. My spiritual roots drew life and nourishment from the river, and many times I felt it must surely be time for the next step. But the Lord continued to move on our hearts, telling us to stand where we were and watch what His Spirit was doing.

Many times God brings His people to the waters of revival, but when we cannot stand still and let God lead us, we miss the opportunity for revival, and we draw back into disappointment and confusion. Disappointed and confused Christians seldom see any hope of revival.

Those five years of standing still often appeared unfruitful to the natural eye. But those years were a necessary preparation for the ministry that was in store for me on the other side of the river. The fruit was not visible in my circumstances, yet the effects of the flow of revival bore much fruit in my own personal spiritual life. Paul taught this principle to Timothy as he was being prepared for his part in the revival of the first century. Paul said that the husbandman must first be a partaker of the fruit, II Timothy 2:6.

At the end of that time of standing still, God began to add to my ministry. Now our worldwide outreach includes radio, television, magazines, books, tapes, conferences, crusades, and a strong home-based church with a Christian education program from preschool through Bible college.

I relate in retrospect the experiences from which I gained the ability to understand these spiritual principles. I did not know at those times that I was being led in biblical patterns. I was simply trusting God and following the leading of the Holy Spirit day by day. Once I understood these principles, I found it much easier to move on with God and cross other rivers I faced in my spiritual growth.

Stand firm on God's Word

Another step in crossing the river into a new place in God where revival will continue to increase in our lives is to stand firm on God's Word. This is illustrated in Joshua 3:16,17. Here we read that the waters of the river were cut off and the priests, with the ark of the covenant resting on their shoulders, moved into the midst of the dry riverbed.

Two beautifully prepared golden rods were the means by which the ark was carried on the shoulders of the priests in those days. This was part of God's due order for moving the ark from place to place. These rods, as all other aspects of tabernacle worship, have symbolic meaning to us as believers. I believe that one rod speaks to us of God's grace and the other of His mercy, both of which are ever extended to us. These two important Bible truths must be deeply rooted in our hearts.

"... out of the abundance of the heart the mouth speaketh."
Matthew 12:34.

If our praises are to truly carry the presence of God, they must come out of hearts established in grace and mercy. Frequently, throughout the Old Testament, when the ark of the Lord was to be carried by the priests, the people were instructed to give thanks and sing, "The Lord is good, and His mercy endureth forever."

Goodness and mercy

It is not enough to have truth resting on our shoulders in a praise service, we must also have the same truth and praise in our daily walk. One foot must stand on the solid truth that God is good. The other foot must stand on the equally solid truth that His mercy endures forever.

The dry ground upon which the priests stood speaks to us of a solid place in God where our sense of security comes from an interpretation of the Scriptures based on the fact that God is not only good to us at the present time, but He will continue to be good to us throughout all time because His mercy endures forever. With God's presence on our shoulders, and our feet planted solidly on His Word, we are in the place where faith can grow and miracles can happen.

Many wonderful things occur when our faith becomes fixed on God's Word: Satan's threats do not disturb us; we stand on the Word.

"...greater is he that is in you, than he that is in the world,"
I John 4:4.

Our failures do not defeat us; we stand on the Word.

"Rejoice not against me, O mine enemy: when I fall, I shall arise...," Micah 7:8.

A friend turning against us does not destroy us; we stand on the Word.

"...and there is a friend that sticketh closer than a brother,"
Proverbs 18:24.

No circumstance or trial dismays us; we stand on the Word.

> *"And we know that all things work together for good to them that love God, to them who are the called according to his purpose,"* Romans 8:28.

World conditions do not bring fear to our hearts; we stand on the Word.

> *"Fear not, O land, though the enemy has done monstrous things, the Lord will do marvelous things."*
> Joel 2:20,21 NKJV, paraphrased.

Even those who say that we will never have another great revival do not cause us to lose hope; we stand on the Word.

> *"Be glad and rejoice in the Lord your God, for He will give you the former and the latter rain in the same month,"*
> Joel 2:23, paraphrased.

The principle of standing firm on God's Word must be applied more and more as we prepare to cross over into the greater things God has in store for our generation. Many of us who are seeking revival have seen the mighty hand of God at work in our lives and know that He has a plan for revival in this generation. Yet we keep wavering. We keep asking God for more signs. What we truly need is to settle down on the Word of God and know that God will send another revival because His Word is forever settled in heaven. He is good, and his mercy does endure forever.

To experience greater manifestations of God's power we must learn to keep looking at the Word of God through eyes of grace and mercy. Standing on God's Word is never a waste of time. It is always an investment in greater things to come.

The Waiting Harvest

Every spiritual principle involved in our Bible example of crossing the river is designed to bring us into the waiting harvest. Revival is always a time of reaping the harvest, and the harvest is in two areas. First, as believers, we reap blessings on a personal basis. God will see to it that we are blessed above and beyond anything we can ask or think, Ephesians 3:20. The second, and by far the greater harvest of revival time, is the harvest of the multitudes of lost souls.

The fact that great multitudes are saved during times of revival, numbers of people above and beyond what we normally experience, is illustrated by Joshua 3:15 where we find that the river Jordan overflowed its banks throughout harvest time. We must remember that the water represents the Holy Spirit, and therefore the Spirit of God will be overflowing all boundaries throughout harvest time. Normally, the river of God flows within its banks and only those who come to the river and get in will be blessed, but in revival times the waters spread throughout the community, sweeping many souls into the kingdom of God. When I speak of revival, I picture the river of God overflowing its banks in every direction, causing a great harvest throughout the earth.

In recent winters, there were floods throughout the Midwest, and many Midwestern rivers overflowed their banks. While flying across the nation, I could see that the Mississippi River had spread for miles and miles and reached into city after city. The Lord used that scene to open my understanding to this spiritual lesson. He caused me to see how none of the people in those cities prayed for the river to come into their houses. Yet when the rains came, the river overflowed and reached millions of people who did not ask for it.

Even so, as the rain of the Spirit continues to fall, there will be a rising of the Spirit of God throughout the land. People who have never given God a thought will find themselves overcome by the presence of God even as it was in the days of the revivalists of centuries past, and they will fall on their knees and accept Jesus as Savior. All truly great revivals have shared this phenomenon.

God gives every generation many opportunities to cross the river and enter into revival, for the Lord is merciful and His truth endures to all generations. The good things of today are leading us into greater things for tomorrow.

The Church of our generation has been camped for a long time in the lodging place where new principles are learned. Many have taken their stand on the Bible principle that God is good and His mercy endures forever, and they are expecting the greatest revival in history.

We are getting ready to cross over into a realm where the blessings and miracles of God will come upon the multitudes in the harvest fields of earth. We, the believer-priesthood of this generation, are standing with our feet in the waters of a new revival — perhaps the greatest revival of history. Let us move on with God's plan and carry the ark of His presence through the river and into the waiting harvest.

Questions for this chapter on page 219

. . . but the knowledge of God must shine generally throughout all the world and every one must be partaker of it, we must take pains to bring all them that wander out of the way to the way of salvation: and we must not only think upon it for our life time, but for after our death.

John Calvin, *Sermons on the Epistles of St. Paul to Timothy and Titus, 1579,*

Thus the Spirit of God came upon Othniel; with wisdom for government and courage for war, Judges 3:10. Thus God sent his Spirit on Cyrus, his anointed, to qualify him for the mighty work he was to effect, Isaiah 45:1 . . . Thus also Zerubbabel was enabled to build the temple, notwithstanding the strongest opposition, that it might be evident to all, that the work was effected, not by might, nor by power, but by the Spirit of the Lord, Zechariah 4:6.

John Owen, *The Holy Spirit,* 1616–1683,

Chapter 14

THE PEOPLE OF HIS PRESENCE

Christians of every generation have looked upon Christ's return as the ultimate hope for the Church and the world. The hope of Christ's millennial reign, when He brings with Him the saints of all ages, is threefold:

➤ The devil will be bound.

➤ The saints of God will rule with a rod of iron.

➤ Righteousness will flourish in the earth, causing sin to cease among the nations.

The hope of revival is similar. God has promised that His people will inherit His kingdom in the here and now, and has allotted them ample authority to do the job well. This authority includes total power over all the power of the enemy. He has also commissioned his people to go into all the world and preach the gospel to every creature.

Spiritual Maturity

The exercise of our authority and our resulting ability to carry out His commission is determined by our spiritual maturity. The degree of our individual maturity and the combined unity of maturity throughout the Body of Christ determines the degree to which we will subdue the powers of the world, the flesh and the devil.

The major difference between times of revival, when the knowledge of the glory of the Lord fills the earth, and times of spiritual coldness, when darkness is upon the face of the people, is evidenced in the maturity level of God's people. The greater number of mature, obedient saints who arise and shine, the greater the glory of the Lord will fill the earth. The fewer who arise and shine, the greater the darkness will cling to the minds of men.

While it has pleased the Lord to withhold the ultimate hope of His second coming for nearly two thousand years, He has not left us in darkness. Throughout Church history there have been times of great revival when the kingdom of God was adequately staffed by mature believers whose united efforts brought light and glory throughout the earth.

Every generation can expect revival

Our hope of revival is anchored in God's promise to never leave us nor forsake us and to be with us even unto the end of the world. Therefore, regardless of world conditions, or of how long the Lord may yet delay His second coming, every generation can expect revival. God works in every generation to staff His Church with believers who manifest His presence in a mature way.

The questions must be asked of those who think there is no hope for revival in our generation:

➤ Has not God given us all power and commanded us to do all things which He, Himself, did? and greater works?

➤ Are we not only to pray for His kingdom to come, but also for His will to be done on earth as it is in heaven?

What causes all things to be done according to His will in heaven? The power of His presence. What will cause all things to be done on earth according to His will? The power of His presence. Truly it is the power of His presence that creates a willingness in the hearts of men to do the will of God.

The power of His presence

"Thy people shall be willing in the day of thy power...," Psalm 110:3.

The central theme of the gospel is Christ in the believer, the hope of glory. Colossians 1:27. It is when the Holy Spirit is at work in our hearts that the presence of Christ in us is demonstrated to the people of the world. John, Chapters 14-17. Thus, the people who allow God's presence to be demonstrated in their lives are the people who are used to bring revival.

Light of the world

"Ye are the salt of the earth...ye are the light of the world...," Matthew 5:13,14.

The light of the world is His presence shining forth from our lives. The presence of Christ abiding in us has the same preserving effect on the nations as salt does on meat, preserving and keeping the world from total corruption and self-destruction. But in times of sweeping revival, when the presence of Christ shines forth in the Church, the world is not only preserved from self-destruction, but the light of the gospel opens the eyes of blinded humanity and multitudes turn to the Lord and are saved.

Manifestation of God's presence

I Corinthians 12 speaks frequently of the manifestation of the presence of God through His Spirit in each believer, and says that the manifestation of the Spirit is given to *every* man to profit *all*. The Greek word, *phaneroo*, is translated both "manifest" and "appear" in the King James Version. Colossians 3:4 says that Christ is our life and when He shall appear, or be made manifest, then shall we also appear, or be made manifest, in the same power and glory. Likewise,

I John 2:27,28 speaks of living in the continuing anointing, so that we will have confidence and boldness because of Christ's presence in us.

Frequently in the King James Version, the words *coming, appearing* and *His presence,* as in *"...the power of the Lord was present to heal them,"* Luke 5:17, speak of the same work of the Holy Spirit. While the ultimate hope of the Church and the world is the bodily appearance of Christ at the last trump, the immediate hope of the world is revival, a time when God's presence is clearly demonstrated in the lives of His people.

Jesus said that the Holy Spirit would take the things of Christ and reveal them unto us. The manifestation of the Spirit is always for the revealing of Christ. Just as Jesus said in John 14:9, *"He that has seen [the manifestation of the Spirit in] me has seen the Father;"* so, in essence, Jesus said, "He that has seen the manifestation of the Spirit in you, my people, has seen me." Thus we have coined the phrase, *the people of His presence.*

Walk in the Spirit

The people of His presence are people of revival. They are a people who have rent the veil of flesh and who walk in the Spirit. So often when we think of walking in the Spirit, or walking in the power of faith, we consider only the personal benefits experienced by believers. The greater benefit of walking in the Spirit is that in so doing we cause the glory of the Lord to shine forth upon the nations. And the promise of Isaiah 60 is that multitudes including the kings of the earth, will come to Christ when God's glory is seen in us.

Preparation for the greatest revival in history is gaining momentum as believers throughout the world are being changed day by day, as God takes us from glory to glory. As we grow by degrees, the exact image of the person and presence of Jesus Christ will eventually be seen in us. As He is, so are we in this present world.

Love of God poured out

Revival is nothing more or less than the love of God being poured out upon the masses of humanity. I John 3:1 says that God, in calling us His sons, has shown the greatness of His love. Verse 2 then says that even though we are the sons of God right now, it is not yet fully evident what we shall be. As we grow and learn to walk in the power of His presence, we shall be like Him.

I John 3:8 says that the reason the Son of God appears in His glory among men is to destroy the works of the devil. The love of God poured out through mature believers breaks Satan's power and opens the eyes of those he has blinded, II Corinthians 4:1-7.

We often ask God to do a work in our lives and yearn to see the works of His hands, yet fail to realize that we need more than the works of His hands; we need His total presence.

> *"...in thy presence is fulness of joy* [light, health, and peace]; *at thy right hand there are pleasures for ever-more,"* Psalm 16:11

Never can we over-emphasize that we need the Blessor more than the blessing, the Giver more than the gifts, and the Lord, Himself, more than the laws that proceed from His throne. Without Christ, we can do nothing.

> *"For in him we live, and move, and have our being...,"*
> Acts 17:28.

Seek God's face

In David's generation, God's presence was manifested in such mighty ways that Israel conquered all her enemies. David was truly one of the people of God's presence. He was totally committed to seeking God's presence, and he desired above all else to dwell in God's temple and behold the shining forth of His glory.

When David was seeking God's help to deliver Israel from their enemies and establish a kingdom of peace and righteousness, God's answer to David's plea for help was, "Seek my face," Psalm 27:8.

David replied, "I will seek thy face." Careful study of this scripture shows us that *God's face* refers to His manifested presence.

David's desire at the time of his prayer was for God to do something about his enemies, whom he described as false witnesses, those who breathed out cruelty, and those who had come to destroy him. David wanted God to remove these enemies from his life. God's response to David, however, was, "Seek my face — my manifested presence in your life — and your enemies will be put in their place."

Victory in battle

Psalm 18 tells how the Lord became David's light, and how all of his darkness was illuminated in God's presence. As a result of being in God's presence, the divine decree concerning his rights and privileges went forth from God's throne, and David received instructions that taught him to be skillful in warfare and gain victory on the battlefield.

All revivals are a result of God's presence giving such life, light and understanding to His people that they are then enabled to go forth in His power and defeat every enemy. While many are praying for God to either take them out of this world or take their enemies out of their lives, the Spirit of God is whispering, "Seek my face. Seek my presence."

Possess the land

Moses experienced a face-to-face work of God in his life while he was in the mountain of God. At that point, Moses realized that neither he nor the people could go in and possess the land and bring revival without God's presence. Moses said, *"...If thy presence go not with me, carry us not up hence,"* Exodus 33:15.

The promised land that lay before Israel speaks to us of God's promise of revival in our generation. The opportunity is always before us and the promise is always sure. Yet without God's presence going before us, we will never go in and possess the land.

Not law, but grace

Was the presence of God to be obtained in Moses' day by keeping the law? by doing good to be good? by gaining God's approval by the performance of works? No. Even then, God's presence was manifested because of His grace, as Exodus 33:13 clearly shows.

We must learn, as did Moses, that God's presence is not manifested through the works of the law, but through grace. Moses did not say, "If you are pleased with the way we have kept your law, let your presence be manifested." He said, "If we have found grace in thy sight, let thy presence go before us."

God's answer to Moses was, "My presence shall go with thee and I will give thee rest. Thou hast found grace in my sight."

Moses replied, "I beseech thee, show me thy glory." See Exodus 33:14-18.

God's glory

As God revealed His glory to Moses, he showed him four aspects of His glorious presence. First, He showed Moses all His goodness (His provisions). Then, He showed Moses His name (by calling upon His name, we receive the provisions). Then, He showed Moses His nature as He said, "I will show my mercy." Finally, He showed Moses a place in the cleft of the rock where Moses would be covered over by the hand of God. (This speaks of that place where we are kept in the secret of His presence.)

No wonder Moses' first thought, after Israel's miraculous crossing of the Red Sea, was to prepare a place for God to dwell among them so that His presence would always be with them and assure their good success.

Today, those who are discouraged and feel there cannot be a mighty revival because so many have turned their backs to the law of God need, as Moses, to rediscover the working power of God's grace. The apostle Paul knew this principle well, and he said, "*...where sin* [law breaking] *abounded, grace did much more abound,*" Romans 5:20.

If God would have dealt with Israel according to their sins, he would have cut off that whole generation and He would not have answered Moses' prayer for mercy. But Moses understood that the grace of God was greater than the condemnation of the law. He asked for mercy and received not only grace but God's promise that His presence would go before them.

Many believers are so legalistic, looking only on the outward appearance, that they find it impossible to believe that God's presence could be manifested in places where flagrant disregard for God's law is on every hand, much like it was in the day of Eli. See I Samuel 2-4.

Eli and Samuel

In Eli's day, the light of God's glory had almost gone out. Conditions were so bad outside Israel's borders that surrounding nations were raiding the various communities and threatening to make slaves of all the people. And within the nation, conditions were so bad that Eli's sons were not only incorrigible but were guilty of sacrilegious acts in the house of God. Eli had no hope for a fresh move of God in his time. He sat blindly waiting for death as his escape, unable to see that when sin abounds, it is time to expect a new move of God and allow the grace of God to abound above and beyond the sin of the people.

The grace of God could not be limited by Eli's blindness. Lest the light of God's presence go out, He raised up Samuel. For 40 years, revival fire burned with the light of God's presence in Samuel's heart. Samuel's ministry was a time of preparation for a greater revival in the next generation. True revivals aren't born from legalism or our good works; they flow from God's goodness and grace.

Isaiah's prayer

Isaiah prayed that God would open the heavens and come down so that the mountains would flow down at His presence, Isaiah 64:1-3. He prayed that, as a melting fire that burns and causes the waters to boil, God would make His name known to His adversaries so that the nations would tremble at His presence. Isaiah made his plea yet stronger by asking that it might be in their time as it had been before when God had performed great and awesome things which they had not expected. Then Isaiah went further to declare that God will do more than we have heard of in the past when His presence is demonstrated in coming generations.

> *"For since the beginning of the world men have not heard,*
> *nor perceived by the ear, neither hath the eye seen, O God,*
> *beside thee, what he hath prepared for him that waiteth for*
> *him,"* Isaiah 64:4.

Undoubtedly, the hearts of all concerned believers are stirred with the question: How can Isaiah's prayer be answered?

➤ When will God do these things?

➤ When will He open the heavens?

➤ When will the heavens pour down rain upon the earth?

➤ When will the mountains be moved into the sea?

➤ When will the multitudes be set free?

If my people

The answer to these questions was given to Solomon. The day Solomon dedicated the temple, the glory of God's presence filled the house. It was on that occasion that the Lord, once and for all, answered the cry of men's hearts, "How will revival come?" On that day, God gave Solomon this promise: If the enemy should come into your land . . . if the heavens should be brass. . . if the earth should bring forth a curse. . . if the people should fail to receive any of all these blessings. . . then you can recover my presence and once more walk in all the goodness that my hand provides by remembering and obeying this word:

> *"If my people* [the people of my presence], *which are called*
> *by my name, shall humble themselves, and pray, and seek*
> *my face, and turn from their wicked ways; then will I hear*
> *from heaven, and will forgive their sin, and will heal their*
> *land,"* II Chronicles 7:14.

The message never changes. To every generation, God's word is "Seek my face." Those who seek God's presence with an humble heart, a repentant mind, and a determined spirit to turn from the ways of man and walk in the ways of God, will find heaven open to them. And when heaven opens, God's glory streams upon the earth, giving light, salvation and life to those who sit in darkness, in the shadows and regions of death, Matthew 4:16.

Open faces

The same message is found in II Corinthians 3:18. When our hearts turn to the Lord, the veil and covering of darkness is taken away, and we all with open faces behold the glory of God in the face of Jesus. Then the heavens open, His presence rushes into our lives, and we are changed; that is, the works of the flesh and of this world system come crashing down. We then appear in His likeness, for we see Him as He is. Truly, we become the people of His presence!

To strengthen our resolve to be a people of His presence and to expand our comprehension of the many mighty works that His presence causes to be made known among the nations, let us take a look at some of the scriptures which speak of His appearing or His presence.

➤ He shall appear in His glory, Psalm 102:16.

➤ He shall appear to your joy, Isaiah 66:5.

➤ There is giving of thanks with a joyful noise and with psalms in His presence, Psalm 95:2.

➤ The upright dwell in the presence of God, Psalm140:13.

➤ His presence is the secret hiding place, Psalm 31:20.

➤ In His presence is fulness of joy, Psalm 16:11.

➤ The divine decree concerning our rights and privileges comes forth from His presence, Psalm 17:2.

➤ The heavens send rain at His presence. The administration of condemnation from Mount Sinai is removed at His presence, Psalm 68:8.

➤ Our enemies turn back and fall at God's presence, Psalm 9:3.

➤ All worshipers of the occult are silenced at God's presence, Zephaniah 1:4-7.

➤ There is no place to hide from God's presence, Psalm 139:7.

No wonder saints of all ages have given all diligence to seeking God's presence. As we learn to walk in the power of His presence and are sensitive to the lordship of Christ in all things, revival will go wherever we go. Therefore, Jesus said to the people of His presence, "Go ye into all the world and make disciples of all nations."

Questions for this chapter on page 221

Now, Christians, the more great and glorious things you expect from God. . . the conversion of the Jews, the conquest of the nations to Christ, the breaking off of all yokes, the new Jerusalem's coming down from above, the extraordinary pouring out of the Spirit, and a more general union among all saints, the more holy, yea, the more eminently holy in all your ways and actings it becomes you to be.

Thomas Brooks, 17th Century Puritan, *The Crown and Glory of Christianity*, 1662

Fly abroad, thou might gospel,
Win and conquer, never cease;
May thy lasting, wide dominions
Multiply and still increase;
Sway thy sceptre, Saviour,
All the world around.

1772 hymn of William Williams

The Scriptures are so far from encouraging us to plead for a diminution of divine influence. . . we are encouraged to expect, hope, long, and pray for larger and more extensive showers of divine influence than any former age hath ever yet experienced . . .when the earth shall be filled with the knowledge of the Lord, as the waters cover the seas.

George Whitefield, Revivalist during the Great Awakening, 1763

Chapter 15

WHAT DOES THE FUTURE HOLD
Before the Coming of the Lord?

Since the first publication of the book in 1986, many of the predictions made in this chapter have already come to pass, which reassures our hearts of yet greater things to come.

Isaiah answers the question: What does the future hold? as he declares that the government shall rest upon Christ's shoulders and of the increase of His kingdom and peace there shall be no end, Isaiah 9:6,7. While one generation is reaping the harvest of the former generation, God is preparing the next generation for a new harvest.

➤ It is written that one generation will declare to the next the great things God has done, Psalm 78:4-6.

➤ It is written that eyes have not seen, ears have not heard, neither has it entered into the heart of man the things God has prepared for them that love Him, I Corinthians 2:9.

➤ It is also written that the Holy Spirit reveals to us new things that previously have been hidden from our eyes, but which were planned for us from the foundation of the world, I Corinthians 2:10.

Not only did the Holy Spirit speak through the people of past generations of the greater things to come upon us, but He is speaking to us today about greater things for the future.

"Surely the Lord God will do nothing, but he revealeth his secret unto his servants the prophets," Amos 3:7.

Greatest Revival in History

Surely God has been intensely preparing this generation for the greatest revival in history. It is said that more people are alive on the earth today than have lived and died from Adam to now. Everything that has transpired in this century is working to prepare the Church to reap the harvest of the earth.

Revival foretold

Many of God's people could testify of the things He has shown them by vision and prophecy concerning that which will take place in coming decades. Others, who have already gone on to be with the Lord, have left us documented statements of what the Lord showed them would come to pass in generations following theirs. Many ministers, including Charles Price, Smith Wigglesworth, and Aimee Semple McPherson, who ministered in the early part of the 20th Century, foretold the greater works God would do in coming generations. See Chapter 3, "Never-ending Revival."

Personal testimony

In the 1950s the Lord began to emphasize to me that the best was yet to come. He showed me visions of some of the works of the Holy Spirit that would transpire in the remainder of the century and on into the next. Over the years, as I have witnessed one move of the Holy Spirit after another, such as the Billy Graham crusades, the growth of radio and television ministries, the Jesus People Movement, the

Charismatic Renewal among historic churches, and the America for Jesus marches and rallies, my faith and expectation has grown. Today, it is evident throughout the earth that we are in the greatest harvest time in history.

In the 1970s the Lord showed me a vision of the coliseum in Los Angeles, which seats over one hundred thousand. It was filled with praising people. But that wasn't all. The football field was also filled with praising people, while up to one hundred thousand, who were not able to get in, stood on the outside. As I pondered this awesome sight, the Lord caused me to understand that this great praise rally was the result of years of teaching and the outpouring of the Spirit upon thousands. I also understood that as revival increased throughout the earth, great crowds of praising people would be common sights.

The Lord also impressed upon me that while the spiritual awakening of the 1970s would touch every city in this nation, yet God had reserved even greater things for the decades to follow. The work of the Holy Spirit would be so intensified in large centers of population that millions would be swept into the kingdom of God."

In another vision — this time of New York City — I saw thousands of prayer warriors reaching out to sustain the falling Statue of Liberty. As they continued in prayer, the Statue of Liberty was lifted back to its upright position and its torch of freedom, which had been dimmed for so long, was reignited with a new flame of holy light.

As we have seen the physical restoration of the Statue of Liberty, so we will also see the restoration of our moral values and Christian heritage from the school campuses to the halls of Congress. While millions rejoiced in the restoration of the symbol of liberty, millions more will rejoice in renewed liberty in all phases of life.

We can expect to see events similar to that which took place in the great revivals of Charles Finney's day, when so many people in the cities were turning to God that the bars closed for lack of business. I believe that revival will reach such a point that many criminals will flee to the hills to escape the convicting power of God in the city. I believe a day will come when a drug peddler in the heart of New York City, carrying a bag over his shoulder filled with all manner of drugs, will cry out, "Who will buy the bag for a penny?" and the voices of many adults, young people and children will be heard saying, "There is no place for you in this city." This will also be true of other major population centers throughout the land.

Not only is America destined for a great revival in this century, but many nations that for centuries have stood afar off from the gospel will be drawn to Christ. Entire countries will do as did Babylon in the days of Nebuchadnezzar, as did the Medes and Persians in the days of Darius, and as did Rome in the days of Constantine. In those days decrees went out throughout the known world saying that all people were to honor and worship the true and living God.

As the 1970s rolled by, the Lord continued to speak of the greater things of the 1980s and the 1990s. He said that revival power would reach such a peak that there would be a realignment of the nations. [*This actually began to come to pass in 1989 with the collapse of the Soviet Union and its satellite countries.*] Country after country, including countries dominated by communism, will be shaken by the power of God, and they will align themselves on the side of Christ and the Bible. Moslem countries will experience great outpourings of the Holy Spirit. In years to come, we can expect that same mighty wind of the Spirit to blow again and again, bringing many nations to the cross of Christ as has already been seen in the predominantly Moslem nation of Indonesia.

Christ will take the pre-eminence in many darkened lands as spoken of in Micah 4:1-4:

> *"In the last days it shall come to pass, that the mountain of the house of the Lord shall be established in the top of the mountains, and it shall be exalted above the hills; and people shall flow unto it. And many nations shall come, and say, Come, and let us go up to the mountain of the Lord, and to the house of the God of Jacob; and He will teach us of His ways, and we will walk in His paths: for the law shall go forth of Zion, and the word of the Lord from Jerusalem. And He shall judge among many people, and rebuke strong nations afar off; and they shall beat their swords into plowshares, and their spears into pruning hooks: nations shall not lift up a sword against nation, neither shall they*

*learn war any more. But they shall sit every man under his
vine and under his fig tree; and none shall make them
afraid: for the mouth of the Lord of hosts hath spoken it."*

The renewal of the '70s and the greater things of the '80s were a
preparation for the "mighty '90s" in which God's plan of restoration
will be fulfilled in a larger dimension than in the past.

It is now a recorded fact in the book *The World's Twenty Largest
Churches* by John N. Vaughan that the largest single church in history
is now leading the way with 500,000 members, and still growing.
That church is Full Gospel Central Church in Seoul, Korea, pastored
by Paul Yonggi Cho. A few others with unusually large memberships
are:

➤ Jotabeche Methodist Pentecostal Church, in Santiago, Chile.

➤ Young Nak Presbyterian Church, Seoul, Korea.

➤ First Baptist Church, Hammond, Indiana

➤ Calvary Chapel, Santa Ana, California.

➤ Deus e Amor, São Paulo, Brazil.

➤ Miracle Center, Benin City, Nigeria.

The list continues as revival explodes throughout the earth. It is
said when communists took over China 30 years ago, there were
known to be 10 million believers. It is now reported that there are 50
million known believers in Red China. It is said Africa's conversion
rate is so great that by the year 2000, all of Africa will have turned
to Christ. Truly there is great hope for the future.

This century has been as the time when Jesus broke the bread and
fed the multitudes. Again and again, the loaves and fishes, which are
symbolic of truths emphasized throughout this century, have been
broken and distributed with a fresh anointing and continuing
evidence that Jesus is Lord of heaven and earth. The mighty '90s will
be the season for picking up the twelve basketfuls that yet remain.
We will experience such a coming together and balancing of the
major emphases made in this century that it will be increasingly
difficult to tell which portion of truth was in the first breaking of the
bread or which was in the last; all are coming together in one great
and mighty revival.

In a very real sense, the apostles, in the early chapters of Acts, took the spiritual bread that remained from Christ's ministry, even as they had taken the twelve baskets remaining from the miracle of the loaves and fishes, and they broke that spiritual bread from house to house. All the inhabitants of the city who were hungry ate of the same faith and life from the hands of the apostles, even as the disciples had eaten from the hands of Christ. They had all things in common: one faith, one Lord and one body.

In the coming days of revival, we can expect to *eat* that better portion, symbolized by the twelve basketfuls — that portion which was reserved for the last.

➤ The greatest sermons are yet to be preached.

➤ The largest crowds are yet to be gathered.

➤ The greatest praise is yet to be offered.

➤ The greatest miracles are yet to be seen.

➤ The largest churches are yet to be built.

➤ The total unity of the Body of Christ is yet to be seen.

➤ The greatest harvest is yet to be reaped.

The best is yet to come, for the path of the just is as a shining light that shines more and more until the perfect day, Proverbs 4:18.

Should the Lord tarry and should His plans include generations yet to come, the things spoken of in this book may well seem small in comparison to the things the Lord will yet do. For it is written that from the foundation of the world, the eyes of men have not seen, the ears of men have not heard, and the hearts of men have not known all the things that God has prepared for them that love Him, I Corinthians 2:9.

Let us close the ranks; let us join brethren to brethren and fathers to children until there is such unity throughout the kingdom of God that revival will be experienced by the whole family of God throughout the earth. For He that rides on the circles of the earth by His name, The Victorious One, is ready to give us total victory and total revival both now and forevermore.

Before Christ comes again to receive His bride unto Himself — before the last reaper is called from the fields to sit at the Father's

table — God's plan for world evangelism will be utterly finished. Not one jot or tittle of His revealed plan nor one thought of His secret desires will be left undone.

The force and power of revival will continue to be felt throughout the earth until that day when the inhabitants of heaven will hear the Father say, "It is finished. All things are fulfilled. Every enemy has been put down. All things are under Christ's feet." Then shall the end come when Christ shall deliver the kingdom to God, even the Father. So shall we ever be with the Lord.

Amen

Questions for this chapter on page 223

WORKBOOK

Revival—Hope Burns Eternal
is used in Sweetwater Bible College and its Sister Colleges
as a correspondence course.

If you would like information on how to receive Bible College credits
for this course, please send the coupon below to:

Sweetwater Bible College
PO Box 5640
Glendale, AZ 85312

Please send me information on how I can take your
correspondence course, Revival—Hope Burns
Eternal by Glenn Foster.

I have the book. _____
I need to buy the book. _____

Name _____

Address _____

City/State/Zip _____

Course: **Revival**

Questions: Chapter 1

1. Quote Mark 16:15 _____
   _____

2. God's plan has always been to bring _____ nations of
   _____ generation to Himself.

3. The first nation to be a witness of God's saving grace was:

   a. Chaldeans   b. Hebrews   c. Greeks

4. In the New Testament era God's nation of witnesses include
   _____ _____ _____ _____ _____

5. **Last days** and **last things** mean the same. True___ False___

6. Arab and Moslem nations are included in God's promise to pour
   out His Spirit upon all flesh.   True___ False___

7. According to Proverbs 29:18, people perish when there is _____
   _____.

8. The word "terrible" as used in Joel 2:31 means:
   a. wonderful & notable   b. dark & gloomy
   c. sinful & perverted

9. Those who retain the faith during times of spiritual backsliding
   and confusion are called:
   a. believers   b. remnant   c. faithful

10. Quote Colossians 1:27 _____
    _____
    _____
    _____

11. The word "Jehoshaphat" means the place where _____
    sits to _____

12. Quote Romans 5:20: _____
    _____
    _____
    _____

13. Name the seven Jehovah covenants and scripture references:

_____ _____

_____ _____

_____ _____

_____ _____

_____ _____

_____ _____

_____ _____

14. What 19th Century revivalist said: "Do not tell me of the rising floods of evil, but let me tell you of the rising floods of grace."

_____

15. Matthew 4:16 says that the people who sat in _____ saw _____ _____.

16. Isaiah 60:2 and Matthew 4:16 deal with the principle of:
a. darkness and evil of the world b. light of heaven
c. co-existing light and darkness

17. According to Isaiah 60:5, multitudes will be converted to God.
True____ False_____

18. Perilous times come in ____ ____ _____, which is ____ _____ _____.

19. The bible teaches that the world will get worse and worse, making revival impossible. True ____ False ____

20. Quote Haggai 2:9 _____

_____

_____

_____

22. A New Testament text that shows the principle of light overcoming darkness is _____.

21. The author encourages us to prepare for: a. Armageddon
b. perilous times c. mightiest revival in history

Questions: Chapter 2

1. Malachi wrote: *I am the Lord,* _____;
   Moses wrote: I am that I am - this is my _____
   _____; The writer of Hebrews said:
   _____
   _____

2. The periods of peace and prosperity following revivals in the
   time of the Judges often lasted:
   a. 10 years   b. 40 years   c. 75 years

3. Martin Luther, early 16th century revivalist lived in Germany.
   true_____ false_____

4. Luther's primary doctrinal emphasis was:
   _____

5. The _____ was a major
   instrument in spreading revival.

6. A 16th Century revivalist born in France was:
   a. John Calvin   b. John Wesley   c. John Adams

7. In what 16th Century city was a Christian community established
   in which there was no monarch? _____

8. Calvin established: a. clear teachings of systematic doctrines
   b. church choirs   c. Sunday schools

9. What 16th Century revivalist brought revival to Scotland?
   _____

10. What two revivalists influenced John Knox?
    _____

11. During the revival in Knox's day, Scotland went from _____%
    church attendance to _____%.

12. What version of the Bible was completed in 1611?
    a. The Tyndale   b. The Jerusalem   c. The King James

13. What classic book did John Bunyan write? _____

14. Bunyan spent many years in jail for preaching the gospel.
    true _____ false _____

15. In George Whitefield's day (early 18th Century England),
    spiritual zeal had been replaced with:
    a. praise and worship   b. form and ritual   c. social emphasis

16. Whitefield on occasion served communion to how many:
    a. 50,000   b. 5,000   c. 15,000

17. What 18th Century revivalist established the first Sunday
    schools? _____

18. Who was instrumental in the formation of the Methodist Church?
    a. John Calvin   b. John Wesley   c. Charles Finney

19. A sermon titled, "Sinners in the Hands of an Angry God," was
    preached by what 18th Century revivalist? _____

20. What important document was penned by men who were greatly
    influenced by revivalists Jonathan Edwards and George
    Whitefield: _____

21. Name three colleges which were centers of biblical study in the
    1600s and 1700s: _____

    _____

22. Timothy Dwight, 1795 Pres. of Yale, was instrumental in return-
    ing the school to biblical Christianity. His grandfather was:
    a. Jonathan Edwards   b. John Wesley   c. George Washington

23. Revivalist Charles Finney was part of The Second _____
    _____ in America in the _____ Century.

24. What was Finney's answer when someone asked how he could
    expect a revival when so much evil abounded?

    _____

    _____

    _____

25. Name two revivalists in the late 19th Century.

    _____

    _____

Course: **Revival**

Questions: Chapter 3

1. Name three early 20th Century revivalists: _____
   _____
   _____

2. In 1935 Smith Wigglesworth prophesied to _____
   _____ that he would live to see the
   reviving of _____ _____ _____

3. The prophecy began to be fulfilled in what two decades?
   _____

4. Dr. Charles Price prophesied of a healing revival that would follow his death.   True_____ False_____

5. Dr. Price said that God's power would move in:
   a. well-known ministers   b. pastors and evangelists:
   c. all who believed

6. What revivalist who began in the 1950s has been used to bring
   multitudes to Christ? _____

7. Two waves of revival in the 1960s and 1970s were given the
   names: _____
   _____

8. The prophet Isaiah said the _____ of the Lord would be
   revealed and _____ _____ would see it together.

9. We don't need manifestations of God's glory today because we
   have modern tools of evangelism. True_____ False_____

10. God's glory was manifested in _____ time as millions
    were brought out of bondage.

11. The people of Jericho had heard of God's power and glory before
    Joshua and the people of Israel marched around their city.
    True_____ False_____

12. Signs, wonders, and miracles accompanied the ministries of
    a. Gabriel & Michael   b. Elijah & Elisha
    c. Asa & Jehoshaphat

13. In the days of Jesus and the apostles, the ultimate display of God's shining glory was the _____ of the gospel accompanied by _____, _____, and _____ .

14. Continual revival is like _____ _____ .

15. Short-lived, come-and-go revivals are the normal pattern. True_____ False_____

16. Many Christians think of revival only as a time of special meetings and special emphases. True_____ False_____

17. The author says that he believes the next generation will hold among their doctrinal beliefs a _____ _____ _____ _____ _____

18. The author defines never-ending revival as the ongoing manifestation of God's glory and power among his people. True_____ False_____

Questions: Chapter 4

1. Quote Genesis 8:22 _____
    _____
    _____
    _____

2. God limits himself to man's ability. True_____ False_____

3. God's promise in Haggai 2:19 is that even when the church is as
    cold spiritually as the winter season, there is still _____
    in His barn, _____ in the root of His vine, and
    _____ of a new revival.

4. The changing seasons of seedtime and harvest are:
    a. human timings   b. divine timings   c. climate timings

5. A _____ is a realm with fixed laws governing
    everything under its dominion.

6. The kingdom of God has the power to rule over
    a. most other kingdoms   b. a select few kingdoms
    c. all other kingdoms

7. People who feel that their only recourse is to hold on until the
    end and pray that Jesus will come soon are locked into a survival
    attitude. True_____ False_____

8. A survival attitude produces:
    a. small churches   b. negative thinking   c. evangelistic outreaches

9. What scripture speaks of repeated times of refreshing and reviv-
    ing from the presence of the Lord? _____

10. Quote Habakkuk 3:2 _____
    _____
    _____

11. "Times of wrath" is another way of describing winter seasons
    when little hope can be seen for a great harvest of souls.
    True_____ False_____

12. Exodus 14 tells of a changing of times for God's people. Did they expect this change? Yes_____ No_____

13. Through whom did the beginning of a new season come in the days when Eli was priest in Israel? _____

14. II Chronicles 29 tells of a king in whose life changing times were evident. This king was
    a. Samuel   b. Ahab   c. Hezekiah

15. What king had a dream of a great image that symbolized earthly kingdoms? _____

16. Although times and seasons change, God's plan for His kingdom never changes. True_____ False_____

17. A new season could be called a. a new era   b. a new age
    c. a new day   d. all of the above

18. The author says that we should believe God for greater things than we've dared hope for in the past. True_____ False_____

Questions: Chapter 5

1. Jubilee in many ways is the _____ _____
   equivalent of what we have come to know in _____ _____
   times as revival.

2. What year was appointed as Jubilee in Israel?
   a. 7th year   b. 50th year   c. 25th year

3. Give the book and chapter of a key Old Testament passage about
   Jubilee. _____

4. Quote Luke 4:18,19 _____
   _____
   _____
   _____
   _____
   _____
   _____
   _____

5. The word "jubilee" means: _____
   _____
   _____

6. What key bible principle leading to revival is found in Psalm 67?
   a. prayer   b. repentance   c. praise

7. God led David to establish the way of praise as the everyday way
   of life for His people. True_____ False_____

8. The psalmist said that praise brought _____
   on the battlefield.

9. In Joshua's day what happened at the sound of the trumpet and
   the shouts of the people? _____
   _____

10. In King Jehoshaphat's day who was appointed to go before the
    army of Judah when they went into battle?
    a. archers   b. prophets   c. singers

11. In Psalm 18 David used several symbolic terms; what do each represent:

   thunder: _____

   lightning_____

   coals of fire:_____

12. Daniel 2:44,45 says God's kingdom is like a _____

   _____ _____ _____ ____ ____ _____

13. According to Daniel 7:27, God's kingdom is everlasting.
   True_____ False_____

14. Israel has exclusive rights to the kingdom of God.
   True_____ False___

15. Jesus said that _____ _____ is not of this
   world, and that we must _____ _____ _____ to see
   His kingdom (John 18:36; 3:3-5)

16. Revelation 11:15 declares that the kingdoms _____ _____

   _____ have become the _____ ___ ____ ____

17. According to Psalm 68, who is revived by the "spiritual rain"?
   _____ _____ _____

18. Joel says that God will give us the former and latter rain in :
   a. spring & fall   b. same month   c. two months in a row

19. Jeremiah 34:15-17 said that everyone was to proclaim
   _____ upon his _____ and _____

20. What promise is found in Psalm 100:5? _____

   _____

   _____

   _____

Questions: Chapter 6

1. When the Bible speaks of the glory of the Lord, it is speaking of God's manifested presence.   True_____ False____

2. Name two places where Moses saw God's glory.
   _____   _____

3. Who was king when a visible cloud of God's glory filled the temple? a. David   b. Solomon   c. Asa

4. Paul saw God's glory on the road to _____.

5. We are generally more aware of the supernatural power of God's presence during times of praise and worship.
   True_____ False_____

6. Isaiah 61:4 speaks of the reviving of _____
   and the restoring of _____
   _____

7. One of the best Bible examples of the power of praise is:
   a. Joseph   b. Elisha   c. David

8. Jeremiah 33:11 says to bring the sacrifice of praise into
   _____ _____ _____ _____ _____.

9. According to Hebrews 13:15, the sacrifice of praise is the fruit of our lips giving thanks to God's name. True_____ False____

10. During David's day, praise and worship included many expressions. List three: _____
    _____
    _____
    _____

11. True praise can be offered in spontaneous inspiration or in a skillful, orderly fashion. True_____ False_____

12. Praise void of a heart-felt love becomes only
    _____ _____.

13. The Psalmist spoke from a position of _____ ,
    _____ , and _____ _____
    when he wrote of the importance to praise more and more.

14. Quote Psalm 145:2 _____
    _____
    _____

15. Quote Psalm 119:164 _____
    _____
    _____

16. Psalm 113:3 says we praise God from _____ _____
    _____ _____ _____ to the _____ _____
    _____ _____.

17. In David's day, he appointed praisers to minister to the Lord
    a. in shifts   b. one day each week   c. when they felt led.

18. How long was the period of peace that began in David's time and
    continued through Solomon's?

    a. 20 years   b. 100 years   c. 40 years

19. Quote Ephesians 5:19: _____
    _____
    _____
    _____
    _____

20. What Old Testament prophet did James quote as he referred to
    God's promise to restore the order of worship in the tabernacle of
    David era? _____

Course: **Revival**

Questions: Chapter 7

1. To be asleep, according to Ephesians 5, means to be
    _____ _____ and _____
    _____.

2. One method by which God awakens the church is through judg-
    ments. True_____ False _____

3. Name the two kinds of God's judgments:

    _____

4. Only the wicked dead will appear before the throne for eternal
    judgment to be sentenced and banished. True_____ False_____

5. When Peter said that judgment must begin at the house of God,
    he was referring to _____ judgment.

6. Corrective judgments are God's: a. punishment
    b. principles   c. wrath

7. In Isaiah 42:3, what does God say about a bruised reed?

    _____
    about smoking flax? _____

8. Revelation 10 is a good example of corrective judgments.
    True_____ False_____

9. The word "thunder" in Greek means: _____

    _____

10. Corrective judgments are like: a. fire in a stove
    b. the alarm on a clock   c. an earthquake

11. The seven corrective judgments of Revelation 10 are in the clas-
    sification of scriptures that God applies:
    a. anytime the occasion calls for it   b. during the tribulation
    c. once in each generation

12. Any portion of scripture that is difficult to understand could be
    called a "mystery of God." True_____ False_____

13. What did Jesus tell his disciples when they asked when certain events would take place? a. Pray and fast and I'll tell you
b. I'll send an angel to tell you at the appointed time
c. It's not for you to know

14. Restoration of the kingdom of God is a one-time event.
True_____ False_____

15. Acts 3:19-21 speaks of times of _____
and times of _____ .

16. According to Acts 2:17, God will pour out of His Spirit upon:
a. spirit-filled believers   b. all believers   c. all flesh

17. Distress in any nation can be viewed as a sign that the Holy Spirit will soon begin a new work in people's hearts.
True_____ False_____

18. How many people turned to the Lord under Jonah's ministry at Nineveh? a. none   b. 5,000   c. 200,000

19. One reason why there are times of delay in God's plan to bring all nations to himself is that He needs _____
servants to work through.

20. According to I Kings 10:24, the knowledge of the glory of the Lord filled: a. the temple   b. whole earth   c. Israel

Questions: Chapter 8

1. What kind of a plan does God have for mankind?
   _____

2. According to Psalm 100:5, the Lord is _____
   his mercy is _____; and his truth
   _____ _____ _____ _____.

3. According to Romans 5:20, grace abounds more than sin.
   True_____ False_____

4. When we seek God's viewpoint in any situation, he will show us
   how _____ overcomes _____.

5. In each division of Luke 21, Christ spoke of troubled situations
   and negative forces that the disciples could expect to encounter;
   then he concluded each division with a
   _____ _____.

6. The word "sorrows," as used in Matt. 24 and Mark 13 means
   _____.

7. Hebrews 11 lists those who obtained a good report by faith.
   True_____ False_____

8. Quote John 10:10 _____
   _____
   _____
   _____
   _____

9. Matthew 28:20 says that Jesus will be with us
   a. always   b. when we obey   c. at church

10. The author of *Revival* breaks Luke 21 into 7 divisions. Name
    each division and its corresponding scripture reference.
    1._____ _____

    2._____ _____

    3._____ _____

4._____ _____

5._____ _____

6._____ _____

7._____ _____

11. The regathering of Israel is said by the prophets to be an
    _____ to the nation.

12. The Hebrew word for "ensign" means:
    a. end of the world   b. give a signal   c. holocaust

13. What does Isaiah 60 tell us to do during troubled times?
    a. hide in caves   b. arise and shine   c. protect ourselves

14. When God is in control (Rom 14:17), the fruit of His kingdom
    will be seen in _____
    _____

15. What kind of men will always be able to find a good report?
    a. preachers   b. men of faith   c. old men

Questions: Chapter 9

1. God's plan of revival changes when world conditions grow worse. True_____ False_____

2. Believers whose thoughts are overly occupied with trouble conditions among the nations have a tendency to rule out the
_____ _____ _____, and actually go into a _____ _____ .

3. It is proper to interpret the Bible according to world conditions. True_____ False_____

4. It is proper to interpret world conditions according to the Bible. True_____ False_____

5. According to II Peter 3:9, God is not willing that _____ should perish.

6. The Bible is clear in its declaration that Jesus shall return to earth again. True_____ False_____

7. Can any person know the day and hour of Christ's return? Yes _____ No_____

8. Could an angel from God tell someone on earth when Christ will return? Yes_____ No _____ Maybe _____

9. Does Christ know when He will return? _____

10. Each time someone sets a date for Christ's return and it fails, the results are:
    a. loss of belief in the validity of the Bible
    b   believers become disillusioned
    c. multitudes in the world look upon Christians as foolish
    d. all of the above

11. The author lists seven unscriptural theories about Christ's second coming. Name each:
    1. _____
    2. _____
    3. _____
    4. _____

5. _____

6. _____

7. _____

12. The Bible warns Christians not to base religious teachings on stars and planets. True_____ False_____

13. Doctrines of deduction cannot hold the same authority as an actual statement of Scripture. True_____ False_____

14. The book, *The Jupiter Effect,* published in the later 1970s referred to a _____
_____

15. Did the authors of *The Jupiter Effect* link their theory to either the end of the world or the second coming of Christ? _____

16. Who took the basic theory of the *Jupiter Effect* and linked it to Christ's second coming and the end of the world?
a. sincere but uninformed Christians   b. astronomers
c. science teachers

17. What did the author of *Jupiter Effect* say about their theory in 1980? _____

Questions: Chapter 10

1. Name the two types of revivals the author discusses.

   _____

   _____

2. Ezra and Nehemiah repaired the walls of the city of God in their generation. True_____ False_____

3. Ezra and Nehemiah repaired both _____ and _____ breaches in their day.

4. A breach occurs in the spirit when people fail to follow God's ways. True_____ False_____

5. In the Old Testament era God's presence was only manifested among His people for _____ _____ of time and in _____ places.

6. During which king's reign were many spiritual breaches repaired? a. King Solomon   b. King David   c. King Ahaz

7. What great Bible truth was emphasized during the Reformation in the 16th Century?

   _____

8. What Bible doctrines were emphasized in the ministry of the Wesley brothers in the 18th Century? _____ and _____

9. At the turn of the 20th Century, what two areas of Bible truth were emphasized? _____ and _____

10. In the 1940s and '50s, the church experienced revivals emphasizing God's healing power. True_____ False_____

11. The renewal of the 1960s and '70s brought a restored emphasis on _____ and the

    _____

12. Did any of these revivals do a complete work of restoration? _____

13. In Isaiah 58:12, what kind of places does God promise to build up? _____

14. Isaiah 58:12 speaks of raising up the foundations of many generations. True___ False____

15. What has often happened following a time of revival when God restored certain Bible truths?
    a. other equally important truths are excluded
    b. people built denominations around them   c. both a & b

16. The word "breach," (Num. 14:34), carries the idea of a break in relationship and making of no effect. True____ False____

17. In the author's personal example, he says that God taught him the importance of moving from one administration of the Spirit to another in the realm of
    a. prophecy   b. healing   c. church administration

18. II Samuel 6 tells the story of David's unsuccessful attempt to bring the ark of God to Jerusalem. Why was the man named Uzzah killed?   a. he was sinful   b. he hadn't prayed that day c. he ignored God's due order

19. While the ark remained in the house of Obededom for three months, what happened there?
    a. crops failed   b. God blessed them   c. many people died

20. What Old Testament man was used by God to stand in the breach, or gap? _____

21. Man-in-the-gap revivals last only as long as the _____ lasts and go only where the _____ goes.

22. Name a 20th Century example of a man- or a woman-in-gap ministry? _____

23. What other type of ministry flourishes in the breach?
    a. judgment   b. Balaam   c. women's

24. What two godly qualities are required to keep us from walking in the breach with a Balaam attitude? _____ __and

_____

Questions: Chapter 11

1. Ezra 9:8 says that God has promised to _____ _____
   _____ and _____ _____
   _____ _____ .

2. Psalm 138:7 says God will _____ us in the midst of
   _____ .

3. Habakkuk 3:2 says God will _____ us in times of
   _____ .

4. In Isaiah. 60:2, God's solution for overcoming darkness is:
   a. repentance   b. praise   c. God's glory seen upon his people.

5. What word is used in Isaiah 60:5 to describe the number of
   people who will be converted to God?
   a. many   b. few   c. abundance

6. The healing of nations comes through the combined ministries of
   _____ and _____ .

7. Joseph's ministry brought healing to both Israel and
   _____ , the just and the_____ .

8. Revival power under Moses' ministry was accompanied by
   signs, wonders and miracles. True_____ False_____

9. Who did God use to lead the children of Israel into the promised
   land? a. Moses   b. Joshua   c. David

10. What drove Hannah to the place of prayer? _____
    _____
    _____

11. How did God answer her prayer? _____
    _____
    _____

12. What King of Israel passed on a strong example of how revival is
    possible in every generation?
    a. Solomon   b. David   c. Jehoshaphat

13. What King and Queen ruled in Jerusalem but did not follow God's ways?   a. David & Bathsheba   b. Ahab & Jezebel c. Solomon & Sheba

14. What prophet of God killed 400 prophets of Baal?_____

15. In Elijah's day, how many intercessors did God say had never bowed to Baal? a. 70   b. 700   c. 7,000

16. Whose prophetic ministry was birthed in a most unique prayer chamber? _____

17. Who was a powerful intercessor and prophet when God's people were in Babylon? _____

18. Name four prophetic ministries instrumental in rebuilding Jerusalem and the temple. _____

_____

19. The increase of evil in a nation is a sign that:
    a. God has turned the people over to the devil
    b. There is a great need for intercessors
    c. The end is near

20. Who is the great intercessor mentioned in Isaiah 59:16?

_____

21. Our hope for revival is rooted deeply in God's

_____ nature and His
_____ Word.

Questions: Chapter 12

1. In order to be in unity with others we must first be in union with God. True_____ False_____

2. In Christ's prayer for us to be in unity, he said the result would be that people would know we are _____ _____ and the world will believe that the _____ sent the _____.

3. Christ's prayer for us to be one was first answered in his death, for when he died _____ _____ died with him. (II Cor. 5:14)

4. We remain one in the Spirit because Christ cannot be divided. True_____ False_____

5. What does Ephesians 4:3 tell us to do in regards to unity?
   _____
   _____

6. According to Psalm 133, what has God commanded to take place when we dwell in unity? a. blessing   b. power   c. riches

7. The "precious ointment" spoken of in Psalm 133 is symbolic of a ministry saturated with the _____.

8. Zechariah 4 is an example of unity releasing the flow of anointing. True_____ False_____

9. Who was king when David refused to break the unity of the spirit by being disrespectful to a fallen leader? _____

10. In David's third anointing, _____ _____ was united under his kingship.

11. Deuteronomy 32:2 says that God's doctrine drops as _____ and his speech distills as _____.

12. Quote I Corinthians 2:2 _____
    _____
    _____
    _____

13. The apostle Paul said, "Christ is not divided."
    True_____ False_____

14. God's mighty power works in all believers
     a. always   b. at church   c. if and when they ask for it

15. What do the "watchmen" of Isaiah 52:7-9 proclaim?
     a. doom & gloom   b. coming judgment
     c. peace, salvation and glad tidings

16. Malachi's prophecy (chapter 4) says that the hearts of
     _____ and _____ will be turned to
     each other.

17. Which of David's sons was disloyal and caused disunity?
     a. Solomon   b. Jonathan   c. Absalom

18. Dr. Charles Price prophesied that after his death many well-mean-
     ing ministries would _____ _____

     _____ _____ _____ _____ _____

     and put a price tag on _____ _____.

19. Dr. Price also said that this time would come when these prac-
     tices would come come to an end during a sweeping revival in
     the last part of the 20th Century. True____ False____

20. Who, besides Dr. Price, prophesied of a great revival at the close
     of the 20th Century?
     a. Billy Graham   b. Oral Roberts   c. Smith Wigglesworth

Name _____ **219**

Course: **Revival**

Questions: Chapter 13

1. What river is often used to symbolize a time of crossing over into a new dimension of blessing and opportunity? _____

2. Before crossing over the river, Joshua and the children of Israel waited on the banks of the river: a. 7 days   b. 3 days   c. 10 days

3. Progress in the Christian life is measured in segments of growing from _____ to _____ and _____ to _____.

4. Moving into a new realm of God is easy. True____ False____

5. At times we find that faith principles that brought us through in the past are no longer sufficient. True____ False____

6. It is not uncommon to be led of the Holy Spirit into a new place only to find on our arrival that we are facing _____ _____.

7. According to the author the golden rods which were used to carry the ark of God are symbolic of:
   a. life & death   b. grace & mercy   c. Israel & Judah

8. What were the people instructed to sing sometimes when the ark of the Lord was carried by the priests? _____ _____

9. The spiritual principles involved in "crossing the river" are designed to bring us into the _____ _____.

10. During times of revival and reaping the harvest, we can expect, as believers, to reap blessings on a personal basis. True____ False____

11. During times of revival the greater harvest is that of the multitudes of lost souls that are saved. True____ False____

Course: **Revival**

Questions: Chapter 14

1. The return of Christ is the ultimate hope for the Church and the
   world . True_____ False_____

2. A major difference between times of revival and times of
   spiritual coldness is:
   a. church attendance   b. maturity level of God's people
   c. religious freedom in one's nation

3. The _____ of His _____ causes all
   things to be done on earth according to God's will.

4. Quote Psalm 110:3 _____
   _____
   _____

5. Matthew 5:13,14 describes believers as _____
   _____
   and _____ .

6. The manifestation of the Spirit is given to: a. every believer
   b. preachers & prophets   c. spirit-filled believers

7. The immediate hope of the world is revival.
   True_____ False_____

8. Revival is the _____ of _____ being poured out upon
   the masses of humanity.

9. According to I John 3:8, the reason the Son of God appears in
   His glory is to _____ the _____
   of the _____ .

10. According to Psalm 16:11, fulness of joy (light, health & peace)
    is found: a. in church services   b. in prayer   c. in God's presence

11. Quote Acts 17:28_____
    _____
    _____

12. God instructed David to be skillful in warfare and gain victory on
    the battlefield. True_____ False_____

13. What did Moses say about God's presence in Exodus 33:15?

    _____

    _____

14. In Moses' day was God's presence obtained by keeping the law?
    Yes____ No____

15. In Moses' day, was God's presence obtained by good works?
    Yes____ No____

16. God's presence in Moses day was manifested because of

    _____ .

17. When God revealed His glory to Moses, he showed Moses four
    aspects of His presence. Name them.
    1. _____
    2. _____
    3. _____
    4. _____

    _____

18. In Eli's day, when the light of God's glory had almost gone out,
    who did God raise up? a. David   b. Samuel   c. Elisha

19. Quote Isaiah 64:4 _____

    _____

    _____

    _____

    _____

    _____

20. When Solomon dedicated the temple, the glory of God's
    presence _____ .

Course: **Revival**

Questions: Chapter 15

1. According to Isaiah 9:6,7, there shall be no end of the increase of God's kingdom. True_____ False_____

2. What does Psalm 78:4-6 say that one generation will declare to the next? _____
   _____

3. According to I Corinthians 2:9, God has more for us than what we have seen or heard. True_____ False_____

4. Who reveals new things to us (I Corinthians 2:10)?
   _____

5. Quote Amos 3:7 _____
   _____
   _____
   _____

6. The author says that as revival increases, great crowds of praising people will be common. True_____ False_____

7. The author believes that we will see a restoration of our moral values and Christian heritage. True_____ False_____

8. The author claims that a time will come when drug peddlers in our cities will not be able to sell their drugs because no one will want to buy them. True_____ False_____

9. Name five countries where some of the largest churches in the world are: _____
   _____
   _____
   _____
   _____

10. Before Christ comes again to receive His bride, God's plan for world evangelism will be utterly _____ .

Other books by Glenn Foster

The Purpose and Use of Prophecy
The Power of Your Faith
Bible Answers to the Struggle to Live
Liberty - Victory - Jubilee
From My Heart to Yours (by Darlene Foster)

For a current list of available publications, please fill out this form.
Mail to Sweetwater Publications, P.O. Box 5640,
Glendale Arizona 85312.   Or call (602) 978-5511.

❑ Send a list of current publications
❑ Send a tape catalog of Glenn Foster's teachings

Name _____

Address _____

City, State, Zip _____